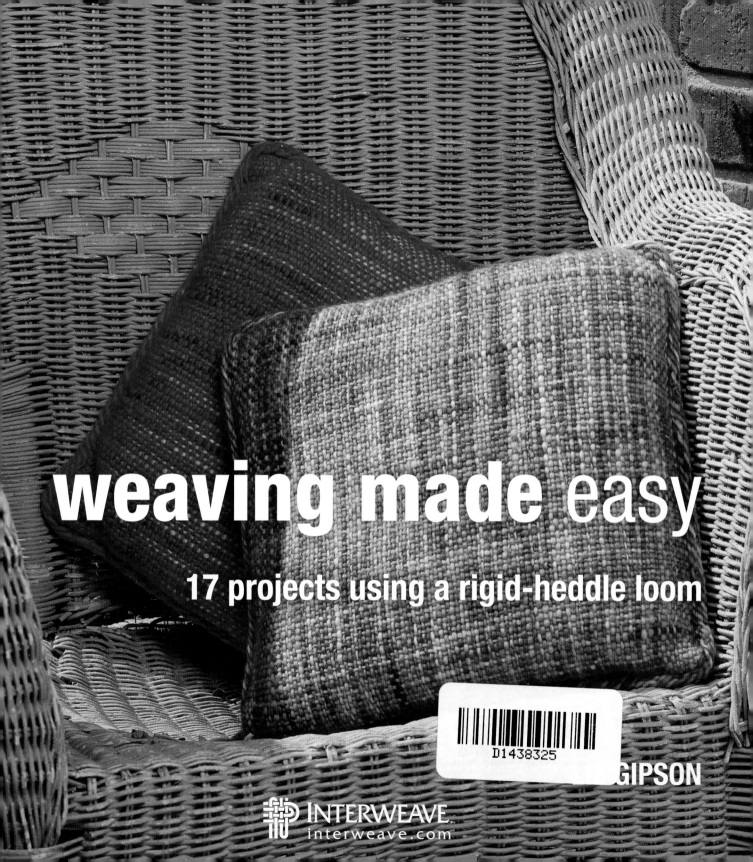

weaving made easy

17 projects using a rigid-heddle loom

GIPSON

INTERWEAVE
interweave.com

Cover Design: Connie Poole
Interior Design: Laura Shaw
Production: Katherine Jackson
Technical Editing: Diane Kelly
Editing: Ann Budd
Illustrations: Gayle Ford
Photography: Joe Coca, except for the following pages by Ann Swanson:
pages 6–22, 24–59, 75, 87, 107, 115, and 119.

Interweave
A division of F+W Media, Inc.
4868 Innovation Drive
Fort Collins, CO 80525
interweave.com

Manufactured in China by RR Donnelley Shenzhen.

Library of Congress Cataloging-in-Publication Data
Gipson, Liz.
Weaving made easy : 17 projects using a rigid-heddle loom / Liz Gipson. --
Revised and updated.
     pages cm
  Includes index.
   ISBN 978-1-62033-680-9 (pbk.)
   ISBN 978-1-62033-681-6 (PDF)
 1. Hand weaving. 2. Hand weaving--Patterns. 3. Handlooms. I. Title.
   TT848.G57 2014
   746.1'4041--dc23
                                2014021640

10 9 8 7 6 5 4 3 2

acknowledgments

To my family and the community of publishing professionals that make writing such a satisfying career choice.

"Easy" is a word that would stop any weaver or potential weaver in her tracks. Easy? Really? Everything is easy if you know how to do it. With the burden of this word in the title, I set about to write a book that would give anyone the tools he or she needs to weave for a lifetime, from selecting yarns to finishing the cloth. I humbly admit that I had blinders on in one very important area—warping.

The method in the first edition is one I love because it's so versatile. Once mastered, there's no hurdle you can't jump. (As a bonus, I like that it takes up less room.) It is not, however, the "easiest" method; nor is it even the fastest. For this edition, I've condensed that option to make space for what conventional wisdom recognizes as the easiest way to warp a rigid-heddle loom. This method can only be used with this style of loom, and it's pretty darn clever.

In addition to adding a new warping method, I've also added a weaver's favorite—projects where you can weave more than one item on a single warp. There are more call-outs and subheadings that make it easier for you to find the information you need.

It's been my privilege to work with so many new weavers over the years. Teachers say this all the time—and we mean it—you teach us more than we teach you.

contents

introduction

Weaving is an enchantress. I'm not sure exactly how I came under her spell. I was fortunate to learn to weave at a young age. All things fiber charmed my imagination. As a child, I would wrap my little hands around the fence surrounding the llama at the petting zoo in order to prevent my grandmother from hauling me away. I read in a book that you could weave with that llama's coat, and I wanted her to teach me how! Working with yarn simply makes me happy, and we tend to stick with things that make us happy.

Weaving, for me, is also a small act of rebellion. We are so far removed from how the items we depend on every day—food, clothing, and shelter—are made. Now, I'm not even close to making everything I wear or all the textiles in my home, but at least I know what it takes to make the fabric that I depend on.

This little loom—the rigid heddle—is the perfect avenue for you to discover what weaving has to offer. Small and portable, it's the ideal blend of ease and functionality. Weaving is one of the fastest ways to produce cloth, and it meshes beautifully with all of your other craft skills. If you sew, you'll be in heaven creating your own fabric. If you knit or crochet, you can combine these techniques for truly unique garments. If you spin, you can create yarns for woven cloth that no one else can buy. If you have never tackled any other craft in your life, you learned all you need to know in third-grade math. Really. It's that easy!

It's time to get weaving, and this little loom is your ticket to the party.

the basics

With every new avocation comes a new vocabulary. Weaving is no exception, but fortunately, there are only a few simple terms to master. When first used, the terms are printed in boldface type; see page 122 for all terms. Woven cloth is formed when parallel yarns that are held taut are interlaced by a second yarn. As a unit, the taut yarn is called the **warp**; individual yarns (also called **threads**) are called **warp ends**. The yarn that travels over and under (or weaves) between the warp ends is called the **weft**; individual weft threads are called **picks**. Woven cloth is made by interlacing the warp ends with weft picks. Long ago, weavers came up with a variety of looms to hold the warp ends taut to facilitate interlacing them with the weft picks.

The rigid heddle is perhaps the most straightforward loom available on the market. The warp ends are threaded alternately through holes in plastic bars (**heddles**) and through the slots between the bars. As a unit, these holes and slots are called the **rigid heddle**. It is also referred to as the **beater** because it is used to "beat" the weft into place. The rigid heddle is lifted or lowered to raise or lower the warp ends to form a **shed** through which the weft is passed. Think of the shed as the space that "shelters" the weft. **Shed blocks** provide a means to hold the rigid heddle in the lifted or lowered position so both of your hands are free to manipulate the weft. The weft is most efficiently passed through the shed by means of a **stick shuttle**, a thin flat piece of wood around which the weft yarn is wrapped. By alternating sheds and beating picks of yarns, the weft yarn passes alternately over and under the warp ends to **weave** cloth.

THE RIGID-HEDDLE LOOM

Cloth Beam Holds the woven cloth at the front of the loom.

Warp Beam Holds the warp threads at the back of the loom.

Shed Blocks Holds the rigid heddle in the up or down position.

Rigid Heddle Apparatus through which the warp is threaded and with which the weft yarn is "beat" or aligned perpendicular to the warp.

Front Apron Rod Where the warp is tied and tensioned at the front of the loom.

Back Apron Rod Where the warp is tied onto the back of the loom.

Stand Holds the loom at a comfortable height for weaving. If you don't have a stand, prop the back of the loom on the edge of a table and rest the front in your lap.

Shed The space between adjacent warp threads through which the weft travels.

Shuttle Holds the weft.

Warp The yarns stretched on the loom.

Weft Yarn that interlaces the warp in an over-under fashion.

Brake Allows the tension of the warp to be released or tightened.

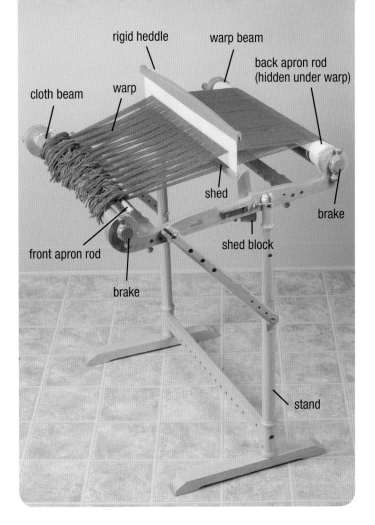

what's in a name?

Although the details are lost to time, it would have been nice if whoever named the rigid-heddle loom had come up with a sexier name. Although "rigid heddle" describes the loom perfectly, it sounds so boring for such an ingenious invention.

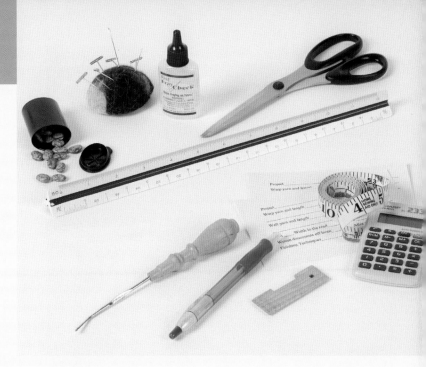

Calculator To help with the basic math needed to determine warp and weft lengths and widths and to figure yarn amounts.

Clamps Used to secure the loom.

Tape measure Used to measure weaving progress—plan to always have one handy.

Embroidery or tapestry needle Used for finishing work and fixing mistakes.

Fray Check A liquid plastic that will safely secure woven cloth to keep it from fraying.

Heddle hook A thin flat hook with an easy-grip handle used to thread the warp yarns through the holes and slots in the rigid heddle.

Inch gauge or ruler Used to determine the thickness of yarns.

Pencil or pen For taking notes as you weave.

Pick-up stick Used to manipulate the warp; also comes in handy to clear the shed when using novelty or sticky yarns in the warp.

Project planning cards or note paper For taking notes.

Scissors For cutting yarns.

Stick shuttle Any of a number of styles of thin flat wood that holds the weft yarn.

Tapestry beater or fork Use to beat the weft (not shown).

T-pins and small glass or plastic jars Used to mend broken warp threads.

Thick paper or warping stick Used to help maintain even tension between layers of warp rolled onto the back beam of a loom.

Warping board Used with the indirect warping method to measure and organize the warp yarn in preparation for threading it on the loom.

Warping peg Used with the direct warping method to measure the warp.

Weighted small glass or plastic jar Used to weight a new warp end that replaces a broken one.

YARNS

Besides the loom, the most important tool for weaving is yarn. Until about one hundred fifty years ago, all yarns were made from natural materials—wool, silk, cotton, flax, yak, cashmere, and the like. Today, yarns are made from all sorts of materials—soy, steel, bamboo, synthetics (these are nothing like your grandma's nylon), and even milk—and most are available worldwide. Add the variety of ways that these fibers can be spun and plied into yarn, and you can get a feel for the overwhelming number of choices available to weavers. To make good choices for your weaving projects, particularly which yarn to use in the warp, you'll want a general understanding of fibers and how they are spun into yarns.

The great thing about the rigid-heddle loom is that it allows you to use a wider selection of yarns than other types of looms.

Fiber Content

Wool, cotton, flax, and silk are still the most popular fibers used by weavers. Each fiber has unique properties that affect how it behaves as cloth. Properly spun, any of them will hold up under tension as a warp yarn. They can be used alone or combined with other fibers in the weft as long as the yarn produces the drape and feel (called **hand**) that you like.

Wool is a protein fiber that is technically defined by its structure, which consists of wavy or crimpy fibers that are covered with microscopic scales (as opposed to "hair," which doesn't have any scales). The word "wool" is commonly used to refer to the fiber shorn from sheep. The scales on wool fiber make it easy to spin and allow the fiber to hold the twist once spun.

The crimp creates air pockets that provide elasticity and insulating properties. Wool yarn "blooms" or swells beautifully during washing. It wicks moisture and provides excellent drape. Llamas, goats, alpacas, and rabbits also produce protein fibers with properties similar to sheep's wool.

Cotton is a cellulose fiber derived from the bolls of the cotton plant. It has high durability but little elasticity, making it an excellent choice for warp. Unlike wool, cotton fibers have no crimp and produce fabrics that are more cool than insulating. In general, cotton is also highly absorbent; however, cotton yarns that have been mercerized (immersed in a bath of sodium hydroxide) have added sheen and are easier to dye but are less absorbent.

Flax, also a cellulose fiber, is made from the flax plant. It has very little elasticity but more sheen than cotton. Flax is very strong and highly absorbent, yet it dries quickly. Yarn spun from flax fibers is called "linen." Linen is considered a luxury fiber and creates cloth that has a cool, crisp feel with beautiful drape.

Silk is a protein fiber that is made from the cocoon of the silkworm. Silk is lustrous, strong, and can take on almost one-third its weight in water without feeling wet, but in doing so, its strength decreases. Throughout history, silk has been one of the most sought after luxury fibers for its luster and drape, making it also perhaps the most mimicked fiber in history. Since the industrial revolution, textile chemists have tried to create artificial silk. Their first success was rayon, and that has given rise to the much more eco-friendly Tencel, bamboo, and other silk-like yarns generated from natural materials.

dreaming in yarn

Do you see yarn and instantly have a vision of what it will be? Have you ever carried out that vision and had it turn out differently from how you imagined? Vision with a bit of experience is the key to making the cloth you want. To do this, it pays to learn a bit about how yarns are made. By learning to spin, I was able to greatly improve my intuitive knowledge on how yarns behave. If you aren't ready to tackle spinning, a little bit of book learning about how yarns are made will help steer you in the right direction.

Yarn Construction
Singles and Plies

Fiber can be spun into yarn of varying thicknesses. A single strand of spun fiber is called a **singles** (note that the plural is used even when talking about a single strand of yarn). Don't be fooled into thinking that all singles are created equal—a singles can range from very fine to very thick. If spun correctly, singles can make excellent warp, but you'll want to test them first (see page 15). A **plied yarn** is made by twisting (or plying) two or more singles together. A two-ply yarn is made up of two singles, a three-ply yarn is made up of three singles, a four-ply yarn is made up of four singles, and so on. It's important to note that the number of plies does not necessarily dictate the size of the yarn—a two-ply yarn made up of thick singles can be fatter than a six-ply yarn made up of thin singles.

Generally speaking, the more plies, the stronger the yarn. Because they don't have the added strength imparted by plying, singles are more susceptible to abrasion from the heddles. Smooth multi-ply yarns generally make the best warp.

finding balance

Weavers often talk about **balanced plain weave** or **balanced weave**. In a balanced weave, the number of threads in an inch of warp is equal the number of threads in an inch of weft. If there are more threads per inch in the warp than in the weft, the fabric is said to have a **warp-emphasis weave**. On the other hand, if there are more threads per inch in the weft than in the warp, the fabric has a **weft-emphasis weave**. If the warp completely covers the weft, the fabric is called **warp dominant**; if the weft completely covers the warp, it's called **weft dominant**. The key to these types of fabrics is the spacing of the warp ends.

Yarn can also be plied to create various novelty effects. Novelties and "sticky" yarns such as bouclé and mohair tend to cling together when forming a shed and can make the weaving process fussy. However, if these yarns are spaced wide enough apart that they don't touch each other, or if sticky yarns are alternated with smooth yarns, they can produce interesting results in the warp.

Yarn Classification

Yarns marketed for knitters are classified based on the **grist**, or size of the yarn—from laceweight at the fine end to very bulky at the thick end. Years ago, *Spin·Off* magazine compiled a chart relating yarn classification and approximate yards per pound based on a variety of sources, as well as the editors' personal experiences. It's worth noting that none of the sources precisely agreed. However, the chart does provide guidelines for how yarns are classified.

Yarn Classification and Yardage per Pound	
Yarn Style	**Yards/Pound**
Lace	2,600 (2,377 meters)+
Fingering	1,900–2,400 (1,737–2,195 meters)
Sport	1,200–1,800 (1,097–1,646 meters)
Worsted	900–1,200 (823–1,097 meters)
Bulky	600–800 (549–732 meters)
Very Bulky	400–800 (366–549 meters)

what do those funny fractions mean on coned yarns?

Yarns manufactured for weavers are classified by size, but they are often expressed by the **count system**, which is based on how many yards are in a pound of yarn of a standard size. This system was designed for industry and not the handcrafter, so it can seem a bit archaic. Each fiber type—cotton, linen, wool—had its own standards that were determined by the trade that controlled that yarn's production. Weaving yarns (often sold on cones) are typically classified by a ratio of two numbers—the numerator represents the size of the yarn with 1 being the thickest, and the denominator represents the number of plies. For example, a cotton yarn classified as 10/2 will have a thickness of "10" and be comprised of two plies. If you know the yardage for the standard size "1" of cotton (which happens to be 840 yards [768 m]/pound), you can find the yards per pound of 10/2 cotton by multiplying the two numbers together: 840 yards [768 m] per pound × 10/2 = 4,200 yards [3,840 m] per pound. Fortunately, most retailers market these yarns with both the count system and yards per pound clearly labeled, so you don't have to remember any standards or do these calculations.

Warp

Now that you understand the fundamentals of yarn production, you're ready to choose yarns for your weaving project. The yarns that are held under tension on the loom are called the warp. Yarns that make the best warp are relatively smooth and tightly plied so that they will hold up under tension and endure the abrasion of the rigid heddle as it moves up and down the warp. Yarns that are fuzzy or loosely spun will tend to fray and break.

To test if a yarn will hold up under tension in a warp, pinch each end of 4- to 6-inch (10 to 15 cm) length between a thumb and index finger and pull your hands apart to create a moderate amount of even tension on the yarn. Then pull your hands apart quickly to "snap" the yarn a few times. If the yarn breaks or pulls apart in your hands, it will probably do the same when put under tension on the loom. Next, hook a bobby pin over the yarn and rub the bobby pin back and forth to mimic the friction caused by the yarn traveling through the rigid heddle. If the bobby pin causes the yarn to pill or shred, the rigid heddle will likely do so as well. But don't despair if you've fallen in love with this particular yarn—you can still use it in the weft, which undergoes much less tension and friction.

Sett

Once you've determined if a particular yarn is suitable for the warp, you'll need to decide how close to space the individual ends in the heddle. The spacing of warp ends in the heddles is called the **sett**. There are three factors that affect the sett of a warp—the number of warp ends threaded in one inch of warp, the size of the yarn used for the warp, and how densely the weft is beat or packed in. While the spacing of the yarns is fixed by the number of slots and holes per inch in the rigid heddle (which, for most rigid-heddle looms, come in spacings of 5, 8, 10, and 12 per inch or their close metric equivalent), you have a lot of leeway in the size of the yarn you choose to use and how firmly it is beat. First, let's look at how to determine a balanced plain-weave sett.

Determining EPI
Warps Per Inch

To determine how a yarn will sett for balanced weave in the size of rigid heddle that you have, wrap the yarn around a ruler for the distance of one inch (2.5 cm).

Wrap a yarn around an inch gauge and divide the number of wraps by two. This will determine a balanced plain-weave sett.

Here's where an inch gauge comes in handy. The notch in an inch gauge measures exactly one inch wide. Wrap the yarn around the gauge for the length of the notch, lightly tensioning the yarn and allowing the threads to touch one another, but not overlap.

Because cloth is made up of both vertical threads (warp) and horizontal threads (weft), the number of wraps represents the sum of the two. To get the number of warp ends required for an inch of balanced plain weave, divide the number of wraps by two. This is the number of ends per inch, and it usually has a margin error of plus or minus one thread.

For example, let's say you've spotted the perfect sport-weight two-ply wool at your local yarn shop. Before you head to the checkout counter, ask if you can unwind about a yard of the yarn (most yarn shops will allow you to do this as long as you wind it back onto the ball when you're done). Pull out about a yard of yarn and wrap it around your inch gauge, winding with even tension and so that the wraps just touch each other without overlapping. Let's say that you were able to wind this yarn 19 times around your inch gauge. The balanced plain-weave sett for this yarn is therefore 19 ÷ 2, or 9.5. Using the margin of error of plus or minus 1, you'll know that this yarn is suitable for balanced weave when threaded through a heddle that has 10 spacings per inch.

Yards Per Pound

If, for some reason you're not able to wind the yarn on an inch gauge, you can determine the appropriate sett if you know the yards per pound of the yarn. The ball band on the ball or skein of yarn will report the number of yards (or meters) and the weight of the ball or skein. With some simple calculations, you can convert this information to yards per pound. For example, let's say the ball band on that perfect sportweight wool reports that there are about 184 yards in 1¾ ounces. (If the yarn

Common Yardages and Setts			
Yarn	yd/lb	m/kg	Sett for balanced plain weave
20/2 wool	5,600	11,300	24
3-ply laceweight wool/silk	5,040	10,150	24
3/2 cotton	1,260	2,535	14
2-ply wool	1,800	3,630	12
2-ply sportweight wool	1,488	3,000	10
4-ply cotton	840	1,605	8

weight is listed in grams instead of ounces—which is quite common with yarns targeted for knitting—you'll have to first convert the number of grams to ounces; there are about 28.5 grams in an ounce.) To determine the number of yards per pound, convert the number of ounces from fractions to decimals (i.e., 1¾ = 1.75). Divide the number of ounces in a pound (i.e., 16) by this number to get the weight, in pounds, of the ball: 16 ÷ 1.75 = 9.14 (rounding up to the nearest tenth). Multiply this number by the number of yards in the skein to get the number of yards per pound: 9.14 × 184 = 1,681.

By itself, this number isn't much help. But thankfully, weavers before us calculated the appropriate setts for a range of yards per pound in a handy chart that outlines the approximate yards per pound (and typically meters per kilogram as well), fiber type and construction, and a suggested sett for that yarn. For this book, we will focus only on setts for balanced plain weave. An excerpt from the sett chart provided at the back of the book is shown above.

Notice that the chart lists yarns with different yardages as having the same sett. Some of this has

to do with the how the yarn is spun or the fibers it contains—yarns of the same size can have different weights depending on the number of plies, how tightly it's spun, and the differing weights of the fibers.

Our yardage of 1,681 falls between a 2-ply wool at 1,488 yards/pound that's listed as having a balanced plain-weave sett of 10 and a 2-ply wool at 1,800 yards/pound that's listed as having a sett of 12. Right away, we can tell that our yarn will work between 10 and 12 ends per inch. Although we don't know the ideal sett (for that we'd want to get a hold of a ball of yarn and count the wraps on an inch gauge), at least we have a narrow range to work with. To help narrow down the possible ranges you'd calculate for the yarns used in this book, I've provided a sett chart on page 125.

Yarn Construction Considerations

When thinking about sett, consider the fiber and preparation of the yarn. Wool yarns spun with lots of air will bounce back after they're released from tension from the loom, while cotton yarns won't. Loose setts are recommended if you want the yarn to full or felt. Setting a yarn looser than recommended for balanced plain

weave will result in a lacy fabric, while yarns sett denser than recommended plain weave will be sturdier.

If you shop for yarns online or from catalogs that cater to weavers, you'll find that many will include information on each yarn's sett and suitability as a warp. Keep in mind, though, that warp suitability is usually based on the amount of friction caused on shaft looms, which is typically much higher than that caused by rigid-heddle looms, and many yarns labeled as unsuitable for warp may be just fine on these gentler looms. If you're in doubt, call or email the yarn source to ask their opinion.

Weft

Warp yarns are just half the equation when it comes to creating great cloth. How the warp and weft interact will determine the look and feel of your cloth. If you sett for balanced plain weave and use the same yarn in the warp and weft, then the resulting cloth will have a balanced weave. Balanced weaves are just one of the ways that you can sett your yarns to get cloth. For instance, widely spaced setts with thick wefts and a strong beat will produce a sturdy rug-like fabric, while a thin weft in the same sett and a light beat will produce drapey lace.

I usually recommend adding ten inches of warp to a project so that it's possible to sample with various weft yarns. (*Note:* For economy or other reasons noted, not all the projects in this book call for sampling.) This way, if the yarn you chose for the weft doesn't seem to do the job, you can experiment with other yarns. It is much easier to swap out weft yarns than it is to rewarp the loom.

Remember that beat also plays a role in how your cloth will turn out. See "Find Your Beat" on page 42 for more information.

These swatches show how various weft colors (shown as yarn butterflies) look when woven with the same yellow warp.

Color in Weaving

Many weavers feel adrift when it comes to selecting colors for a project. We choose colors every day of our lives—while selecting the clothes we wear or determining how to decorate our homes. Yet, choosing yarns for weaving cloth can seem daunting because it's often difficult to envision how two or more colors will interact with each other in the over-under structure of woven cloth. Unlike the simple pairing of a light blue top with brown pants, where each color is seen independently, pairing a light blue warp with a brown weft, where the two interact with each other on a smaller scale and visually blend together, can produce a completely different color. A quick test to see how colors will react in woven fabric is to twist a strand of each together.

I often choose colors with high contrast because they show the interlacements of the warp and weft most clearly. But creating contrast is just the tip of the color-theory iceberg. Entire books are published on this subject, but to be honest, only by weaving the yarns together will you be able to know exactly how they interact. To get a better grasp on how colors work together, try weaving a color sampler, like my friend and colleague Amy Clarke Moore did for the samples on page 19.

Amy chose twenty-six colors of Brown Sheep's Lamb's Pride Worsted yarn sett at 10 epi to weave small blocks of color against a solid yellow warp. She began with the three primary colors—red, yellow, and blue. Then she added value contrast to the mix by weaving one tint (addition of white) and one tone (addition of black) of each primary color. She then moved on to the secondary colors—green, purple, and orange—and wove one tint and one tone of each of these. Finally, Amy used the neutrals brown and gray and wove one tint and one tone each of brown and gray in addition to black and white.

I encourage you to weave similar samples for your own reference on how colors interact with one another in woven cloth. Refer to them when choosing colors for your next warp and weft, and you'll have a pretty good idea of what to expect.

PROJECT PLANNING

Once you have decided what you want to weave and you have selected the perfect yarn, you're ready to figure out how much yarn you'll need for the warp and weft. The amount depends on the length and width of the finished piece, plus extra to account for the yarns traveling in an over-under pattern instead of in a straight line, shrinkage from washing, and to account for the yarn being tied on the loom. For example, let's say that you want to use that lovely sportweight wool used in the example on page 16 to make a scarf with a finished measurement of 60" (152.5 cm) long by 6" (15 cm) wide. A scarf is a good first project because the final dimensions aren't critical—it won't be a problem if the scarf ends up a little shorter or longer.

Determine Amount of Warp

You've already determined that this sportweight yarn will weave a balanced cloth if sett at 10 ends per inch. But, before you'll know how much yarn to buy, you'll need to know how long each warp end will need to be and the total number of warp ends.

Warp Length

For a 60" (152.5 cm) finished length, it follows that the warp will need to be at least 60" (152.5 cm) long. But that's not all. You'll also need to allow extra length for the process of weaving, attaching the warp to the loom (called warping or dressing the loom), and for shrinkage. **Take-up** includes the extra inches "taken up" as the warp threads bend over and under the weft threads (they don't travel in a straight line) and the amount the fabric relaxes when it is released from tension on the loom.

Shrinkage is also a consideration. Fiber content is a big factor in determining shrinkage. If you use a non-superwash wool, you should expect the fabric to lose

more width and length than if you used cotton or silk. Generally speaking, add another 10% for take-up and shrinkage of cotton, silk, linen, and other similar yarns, and add 15% for wool-like yarns.

Loom waste is the amount of yarn needed to secure the warp ends onto the loom. It's length that can't be woven into the project, although it can be used for fringe at each end. Each loom is different, but in general, 24" (61 cm) is sufficient allowance for loom waste on a rigid-heddle loom. This 24" (61 cm) allows for 6" (15 cm) to tie the yarn onto the back of the loom, 6" (15 cm) to tie the yarn onto the front of the loom, and about 6" (15 cm) at each end between where the yarn is tied on and a suitable shed can be made for weaving.

In addition, it's a good idea to allow a little extra yarn so you can weave a sample at the beginning of your project. This is a good opportunity to try out different weft yarns or finishing techniques, especially washing. For example, you can see how the sample reacts to machine washing without inadvertently ruining the woven scarf in the machine. In most cases, 10" (25.5 cm) is an adequate allowance for sampling. This amount will allow for about 5" (12.5 cm) of warp for weaving your sample; the other 5" (12.5 cm) is used to separate the sample from the beginning of your project.

For our example, the total warp length is the sum of woven length, take-up and shrinkage, loom waste, and sampling length:

When doing your calculations, always round up to the nearest whole number.

60" (woven length of project) + 9" (15% take-up and shrinkage) + 24" (loom waste) + 10" (sampling allowance) = 103" total length of each warp thread.

Determine Number of Warp Ends

Next, you need to know how many warp ends you'll need to get the desired 6" (15 cm) finished width. You've already determined that you want a sett of 10 ends per inch (epi). But you'll also need to take into account widthwise take-up and shrinkage. As discussed earlier, 15% is appropriate for most wool yarns.

The total number of warp ends is the sum of the woven width plus take-up multiplied by the sett. For our example:

6" (woven width of project) + .09 (15% take-up and shrinkage) = 6.9" (width in the rigid heddle). 6.9" (width in rigid heddle) × 10 (sett in warp ends per inch) = 69 warp ends total.

Total Amount of Warp Yarn

Now it's a simple matter of multiplying the total length by the number of ends to get the total yardage needed in inches:

103" (total warp length) × 69 (total warp ends) = 7,107".

To convert the number of inches to the number of yards, divide this number by 36:
7,107" ÷ 36" = 198 yards (181 m) of warp needed.

Weft

To determine the amount of yarn needed for weft, you'll need to know if you want to weave a balanced, warp-dominate, or weft-dominate cloth (see page 14). For our example, let's say we want a balanced weave. By definition, there will be as many weft threads—called **picks per inch** (abbreviated **ppi**)—as warp ends (epi). To calculate the amount of weft, multiply the width of the warp in the reed by the picks per inch and the total woven length. Then add 15% for take-up and shrinkage. This is the amount that will be needed to allow for the weft yarn to bend over and under the warp yarn:

6.9" (width of warp in reed) + 15% (take-up and shrinkage) = 7.9"
7.9" × 10 ppi × 60" (total length of woven warp) = 4,740".

To convert the number of inches to yards, divide this number by 36:
4,740 ÷ 36 = 132 yards (121 m) of weft needed.

yarn calculation tips

- Take a photocopy of the project planning worksheet (page 124) and a calculator with you when you're choosing yarn for a project. That way, you'll have no trouble determining how much yarn you'll need.

- To be sure that you have enough yarn for your project, it's a good idea to buy at least 10% more yarn than you think you'll need.

- If you plan to felt or full your project, increase the take-up percentage in your calculations to 30%.

- If it's important to be precise with the finished dimensions of your project and you're at all unsure about the amount of yarn to allow for take-up, loom waste, or shrinkage, test-weave a sample on a short warp before you begin your project in earnest.

warping and weaving

Once you know how much yarn you need, it's time to get those yarns on the loom. This process is called warping or "dressing" the loom. I've included two ways to warp a loom—direct and indirect. Try both to determine the method you prefer.

Don't be surprised if you feel awkward and clumsy the first few times you warp your loom. Just like when you learn to ride a bike or play an instrument, you need to practice to get the hang of it. Many beginners don't know what to worry about so they worry about everything. *I've used italic text to highlight the steps that most often confuse new weavers.*

Once you get the hang of it, you'll be able to warp a simple project in just twenty to thirty minutes!

DIRECT WARPING

Direct warping is a simple method for warping a rigid-heddle loom. Most looms today are sold with all the accessories you need to get the job done. If you don't have these things on hand, you'll be able to obtain them from a loom supplier or improvise with items you can find at a hardware store. Direct warping is great for relatively short warps that don't have complicated color orders.

You'll need a peg that's at least 4" (10 cm) tall to accommodate your warp. You can use anything that's vertical and can be secured to a table. You'll also need to secure your loom to a table or in a loom stand, if you have one. Most looms come with clamps for this purpose. If you secure your loom in a loom stand, try placing a sandbag—available at most hardware stores—on the bottom cross brace to stabilize the stand as you work.

Additionally, you'll need a threading hook, measuring tape, packing paper, warp yarn, and a sturdy contrasting yarn for tying the measured warp.

Setting Up

To begin, secure your loom to the edge of a table or place it in a loom stand. Keep in mind that you'll stand as you work, so make sure that the loom is at a comfortable height. Orient the loom so that the back beam is at the edge of the table.

Next, secure the warping peg either to the other end of the table or to another table, so that it faces the front of the loom. The distance between the peg and the back beam should equal your desired warp length.

Stand behind the loom and place the yarn supply on the floor. Depending on the put-up of your yarn—cone or ball—you may find it helpful to use some sort of container to prevent the yarn from rolling around on the floor.

For direct warping, you'll need a peg, clamps, a threading hook, a measuring tape, scissors, packing paper, and warp yarn.

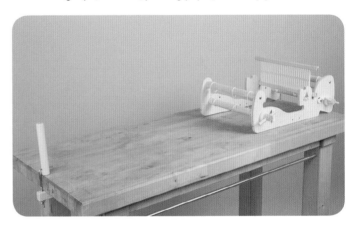

Secure the warping peg the desired distance from the back of the loom. This peg placement will determine your warp length.

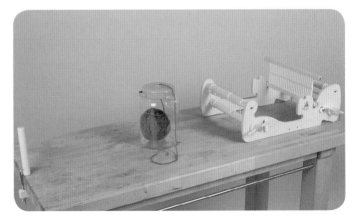

Place the yarn supply in a holder, if necessary, to keep it steady.

Centering the Warp

Place the appropriately sized rigid heddle in the heddle block in the neutral position. To ensure that your project will be centered, find the center of the rigid heddle, measure half the project width from the center, and begin threading in the closest slot. *At this time, you will thread only the slots of the rigid heddle.*

For example, if your project has a weaving width of 5" (12.5 cm), then start threading 2½" (6.5 cm) from the center of the rigid heddle. You can start threading from the right or the left, whichever is most comfortable for you.

Tying on the Yarn Supply

If your loom has a back beam, bring the apron rod over the beam before you start threading. Adjust the apron cords as necessary so that they will hold the apron rod parallel to the rigid heddle and so that the cords come straight back from the rod to the warp beam.

Tie one end of the yarn supply onto the apron rod so that it's even with the first slot that you'll begin threading (use your threading hook to mark this position). A simple square knot is fine.

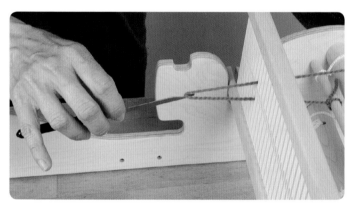

Use a threading hook to bring a loop of yarn through the designated first slot.

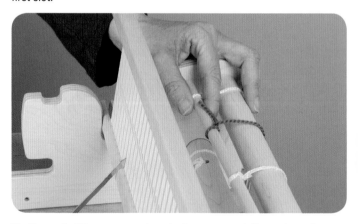

Tie the end of the yarn supply onto the apron rod. If your loom has a back beam, be sure that the apron rod is over (not under) the beam.

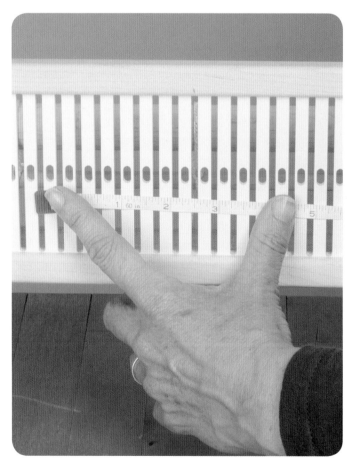

Mark where you'll begin threading the rigid heddle so that the warp width will be centered on the loom. A five-dent rigid heddle is shown here.

Threading the Slots

Use a threading hook to bring a loop of yarn from back to front through the first slot. One end of the loop will be secured to the apron rod and the other end will feed from the yarn supply on the floor.

Pull the loop to place it on the warping peg. *Note:* There are now two threads going through the first slot.

Return to the back of the loom, loop the yarn supply around the apron rod, then feed a second loop through the adjacent slot, working toward the center of the loom. *You are only threading slots, not holes.*

Note: You'll alternate bringing the yarn over the rod on one pass and under the rod on the next pass. This alternation will happen naturally as you work. Just be sure to go around the apron rod with each pass. You'll also want to check that the apron rod hangs free of the back beam.

Place this second loop on the warping peg and continue to work in this manner until you've threaded as many slots as you need for your project width. When you come to an apron cord, simply slip the yarn supply to the other side so you can continue working. When the desired total width is achieved, cut the yarn and tie the end to the apron rod.

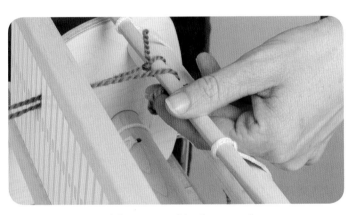

Bring the yarn around the apron rod for the second pass.

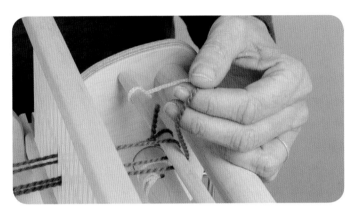

Bring yarn under apron rod for next pass.

Slip the yarn supply to the other side of the apron cord when you come to it.

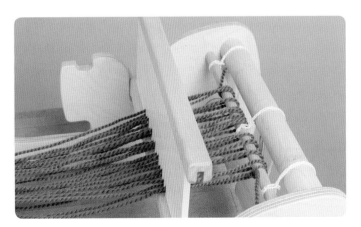

All loops on the back apron rod.

As you work, it's important that you keep the tension on the yarn very light. You want the warp to hang loosely between the peg and the loom. If it's too tight—particularly if you're using an elastic yarn such as wool—you may inadvertently foreshorten the warp and end up with a shorter project than you planned.

Winding On

Tie the entire bundle of warp ends into an overhand knot to keep from inadvertently pulling on an individual end and changing its length while you wind on. Remove the yarn from the warping peg and cut the loops evenly. It's okay to let this yarn fall to the floor (after sweeping up any dust bunnies you don't want in your cloth!).

Next, prepare sheets of packing paper to insert between the warp layers as you wind the warp onto the warp beam. Otherwise, the layers might interfere with each other and cause tension problems as you weave. I like to use sturdy craft paper about the weight of paper grocery bags. Cut the paper into 24" (61 cm) lengths. (I find it easier to manage several short lengths of paper than a single long one.) Don't use paper that's narrower than your project width; ideally, the paper should be about 2" (5 cm) wider than your project. It doesn't matter how much wider

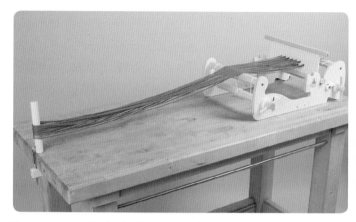

Take care to maintain light tension and let the yarn hang loosely between the peg and loom.

than your project the paper is, as long as it fits the width of your loom. Cut as many lengths as you need to accommodate the length of your warp.

With your loom still secured, stand or sit behind the loom, then wind the warp around the warp beam for one revolution, stopping before the warp winds on top of itself. Slip the paper between the warp layers, then continue to advance the warp allowing the paper to roll onto the beam with the warp. Be sure to add lengths as necessary to maintain a continuous paper boundary between the layers of warp. Watch that the paper doesn't skew and that the selvedge threads don't slip off the edge of the paper.

Remove the yarn from the peg, cut the loops, and tie the ends into an overhand knot.

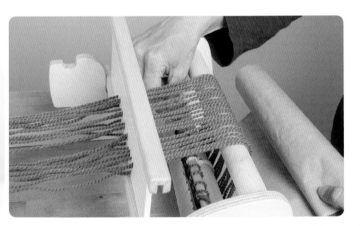
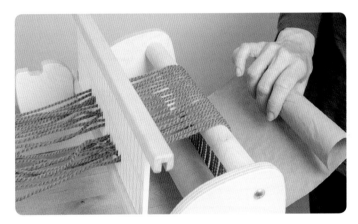

Wind the warp onto the back beam, placing craft paper between the layers.

Resist the temptation to comb the warp ends with your fingers! The less you handle the warp, the better. If you comb the yarn with your fingers, you're more likely to introduce tension differences between individual threads. The individual ends will straighten themselves out as they pass through the rigid heddle.

If you run into a snarl and the yarn won't wind onto the warp beam easily, stand in front of the loom, take the warp in one hand and shake it a few times as you would a horse's reins. If this doesn't take care of the problem, use a threading hook to gently untangle the threads at the front of the rigid heddle.

After a few revolutions during which about 24" (61 cm) of paper has been wound onto the warp beam, stand in front of the loom and pull on the unwound warp as a unit (do not pull on individual threads) to remove any slack in the warp on the warp beam. When about 1" (25 cm) of one length of paper remains, stop winding and lay in another piece. Continue pulling on the slack and adding lengths of paper as needed until the unwound warp is about 3" (7.5 cm) short of the front beam. Untie the knot and give the warp another strong tug to ensure you've taken up all the slack.

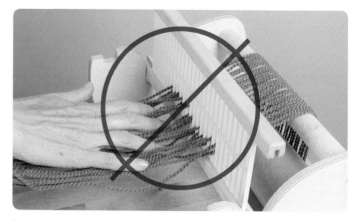

Do not comb the warp with your fingers!

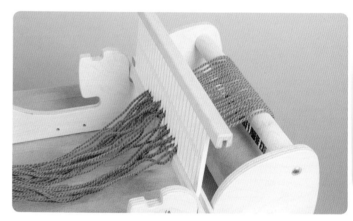

The warp ends may tangle at the front of the loom, but they will pass smoothly through the rigid heddle and onto the warp beam.

Pull on the unwound warp to remove slack in the wound warp.

Place one thread from each slot into the adjacent hole. Here, the thread is being placed in the hole to the right.

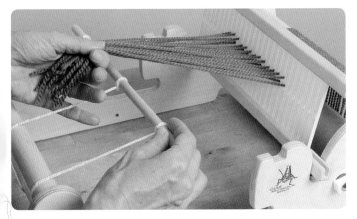

Pull the apron rod into position about 6" (15 cm) beyond the end of the warp.

Threading the Holes

At this point, there should be two threads in each slot. It's now time to move one of those threads into the adjacent hole. Working at the front of the loom from either the right or the left side, take one thread out of each slot and place it in the adjacent hole. It doesn't matter if you place the yarn in the hole to the left or right of each slot as long as you move them consistently in the same direction. *As you place the threads, don't worry if they cross at the back of the rigid heddle.*

Once you've transferred one warp end from each slot, double-check to make sure that there's one thread in each slot and one thread in each hole across the entire warp width. Be sure to note whether the pattern calls for the warp to begin or end in a slot or a hole—and make sure that it's set up that way.

If you have a front beam, pull the front apron rod over it. Make sure that the rod is parallel to the rigid heddle and that the cords extend straight from the rod to the cloth beam, just as you did for the back apron rod. Adjust the position of the rod so that about 6" (15 cm) of warp extends beyond the apron rod. You'll use this 6" (15 cm) to tie the warp onto the rod. Make sure that the brake is engaged at the warp beam to give you something to tension against.

Securing the Warp

Working outward from the center in 1" (2.5 cm) bundles, divide each bundle in half and bring each half over the apron rod and around the outside of the warp bundle. Tie the two parts into the first half of a square knot on the top of the warp to secure the bundle to the rod. Repeat until all of the warp has been tied to the rod.

Working from one side to the other, pull on the tails of the knots to tighten the warp uniformly. Pat the warp to check for loose or tight bundles and adjust as necessary. It doesn't matter how tight the warp is, but it needs to be even. When you're sure it's uniform, tie the tails of each bundle into the second half of a square knot.

Engage the brake on the cloth beam and wind the warp forward toward the cloth beam to take up any remaining slack. You're now ready to weave!

Split 1" (2.5 cm) bundles in half around the front apron rod.

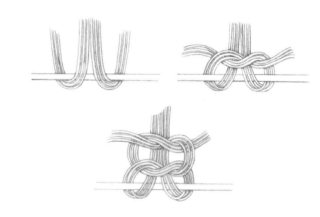

Tie 1" (2.5 cm) warp bundles around the apron rod in square knots.

Tie the two halves into the first half of a square knot.

Adjust the knots to establish even tension across the entire warp width.

Tie the second half of a square knot to secure each bundle.

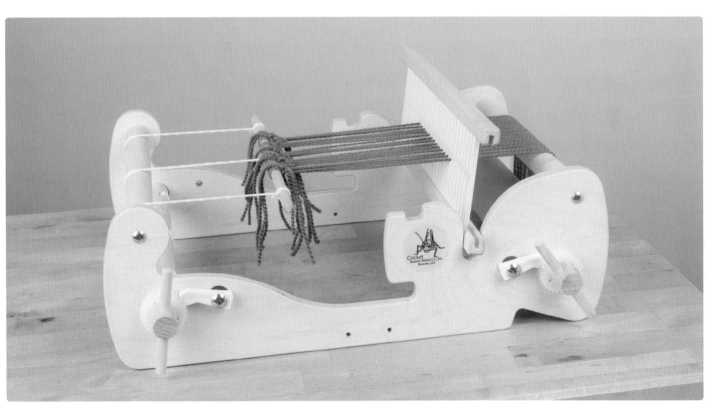
A fully warped loom.

INDIRECT WARPING

You just learned about direct warping, which implies that there must be an indirect method. The indirect method uses a warping board and is handy for complicated threading orders, long warps, and mixes of yarns that have different degrees of elasticity. This method is the one that's used to warp floor looms. The quick introduction that follows illustrates how the indirect method works, so you can try it once you're comfortable with the direct method. For this method, you'll use a warping board to measure the desired warp length.

Winding the Warp

Start by winding a contrasting leader yarn around the pegs on the warping board to map out the path for the warp length you've chosen. You may need to play around with different paths to find the one that fits your length best.

Place the yarn supply on the floor (set it in a container, if desired, to prevent it from bouncing around), and use a slipknot to secure one end of the yarn supply to the peg where the leader ends (see top photo on page 35).

Follow the leader until you reach the first two pegs, which is where you'll make a cross to keep the warp lengths organized and minimize tangles later.

At the first two pegs, wind the yarn over the second peg and under the first, then over the first and under the second. Follow the established path to the last peg, wind the yarn around that peg, then continue back up to the first two pegs and wind another cross.

Continue in this manner until you've wound the total number of warp ends needed for your project. As you wind the warp, keep track of the number of ends wound by looping a contrasting yarn around each group of twenty ends.

You'll need a warping board, leader yarn, threading hook, measuring tape, packing paper, and warp yarn.

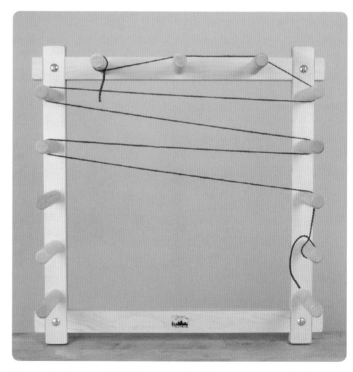

Wrap a leader yarn that's the same length as your warp onto the warping board and tie it to the last peg of a path that equals your warp length.

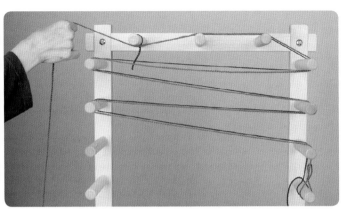

Form the first half of the cross by going over the second peg, then under the first.

Form the second half of the cross by going over the first peg, then under the second.

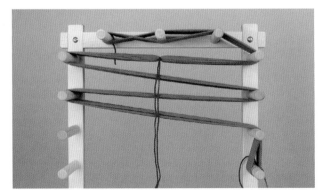

Tie a contrasting choke tie around the warp at the same distance from the first peg as your loom measures from front beam to back beam.

When the entire warp has been wound, wrap the end a few times around the final peg to secure it, then cut the strand. Measure the distance between your front and back beams. Starting from the first peg, use this measurement to tie a choke of contrasting sturdy yarn around the warp.

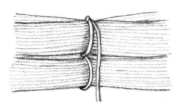

To keep track of the number of warp ends wound, loop a contrasting yarn around groups of twenty ends as you wind the warp.

no warping board?

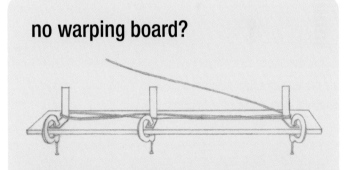

If you don't have a warping board, clamp two L-brackets about a foot away from each other on a stable surface. You will need enough room to extend the yarn to a third secured L-bracket 100" (254 cm) from the first bracket or the chosen length of your warp. You will form the cross between the first two brackets. This process usually involves locking the cat in another room and having someone watch the kids or other individuals who may be tempted to mess with your yarn.

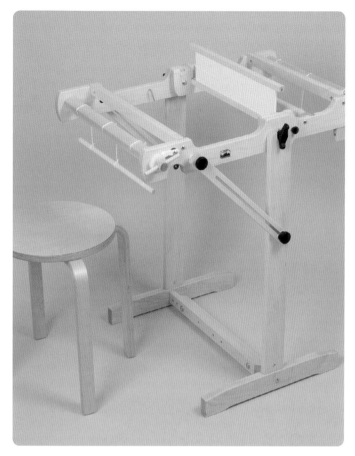

Set the loom in a floor stand or secured to a table with the rigid heddle (8-dent in this case) in place.

Threading the Rigid Heddle

To prepare for threading the rigid heddle, place the rigid heddle in the neutral position in the loom secured in a floor stand or clamped to a table. Have a threading hook, scissors, and a ruler or tape measure handy.

Transfer the warp from the warping board to your loom. Cut the loops at the end opposite the cross (do not cut the cross), being careful not to let the cross

Cut the single loops at the end opposite the cross, then tie them into an overhand knot.

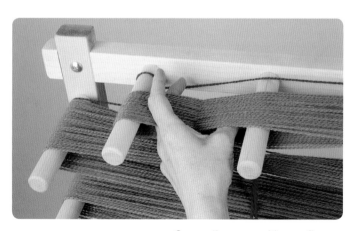

Secure the cross with your fingers as you remove it from the warping board.

slip off the board. Tie the entire warp into an over-hand knot to keep from inadvertently pulling on an individual thread and changing its length while you wind on.

Next, secure the cross in your nondominant hand by placing your thumb in the right side of the cross, your index finger on top, your ring finger on the bottom, and your middle finger in the left side as you gently slide the cross off the pegs.

Tie the choke to the front beam by wrapping the choke tie's tails around the beam and into a square knot.

Carefully cut the loop at the top of the cross so that the ends hang freely. Hold the cross with your palm up and use your other hand to thread the individual ends through the rigid heddle according to your project's specifications, taking care to center the warp as for the indirect method (see page 26).

Tie the choke onto the front beam.

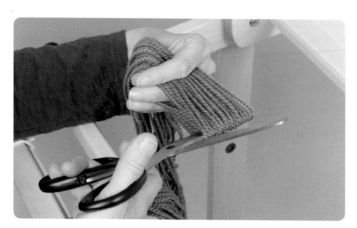
Carefully cut the loops at the top of the cross.

Hold the cross with your palm up.

Use your other hand to thread the warp ends into the holes and slots.

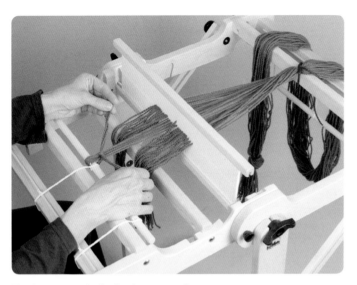

Tie the warp onto the back apron rod.

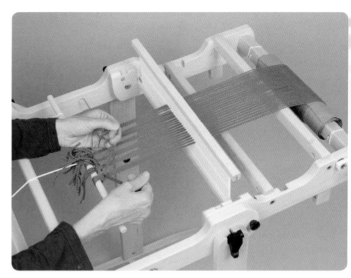

Tie the ends onto the front apron rod.

Winding and Securing the Warp

Working from the back of the loom, tie 1" (2.5 cm) bundles of warp in square knots (see page 32) around the back apron rod, taking care that the bundles are perpendicular to the apron rod.

Cut the choke tie and wind the warp onto the back beam, laying in packing paper as for the indirect method (see page 28) and periodically pulling the warp from the front to remove slack. Resist combing the yarn or warp or fiddling with individual threads—at this point, the loom should do all the work!

Wind the warp onto the warp beam, leaving about 6" (15 cm) to tie onto the front apron rod.

Tie 1" (2.5 cm) bundles of warp onto the front apron rod, working outward from the center, just as for the direct method (see page 32).

in case of emergencies

If you absolutely must put down the warp before you're finished threading the holes and slots in the rigid heddle, be sure to secure the cross in some manner. For such emergencies, I have a steel springclamp attached to my worktable. Its large handles are a perfect place to store the cross so it remains intact until I can hold it again. Place the cross "upside down" between the two handles of the clamp. Allow the loose ends of the cross to dangle free from the lower handle and drape the length of warp on the worktable. Place a heavy object such as a book or another clamp (I have dozens of them around my workspace) on the warp to prevent it from slipping.

Use a steel clamp to secure the cross in an emergency.

The warped loom.

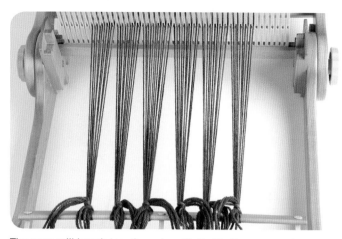

The warp will bunch together when it's tied to the apron rod.

Weave with waste yarn to bring the warp to its full width.

Weaving at Last

Notice how the warp bunches together at each group that's tied to the apron rod. The "real" cloth doesn't begin until these spaces are uniform and the warp is at its full width. It usually takes about an inch or two of weaving, called the **header**, to bring the warp to its full width. You'll want to weave this initial part with waste yarn (you'll remove it before finishing the cloth). The length of the warp between the beginning of the full-width cloth and the knots on the apron rod can be used as fringe—more on that later.

Each pass of the shuttle is called a **shot**. After each shot, the rigid heddle is pulled toward the front beam to align the weft perpendicular to the warp and "beat" it close to the previous weft shot. Because of this action, the rigid heddle is also referred to as the **beater**. The leading edge of the woven cloth, where the next shot of weft will be placed, is called the **fell**. The fell line is perpendicular to the warp threads. Once the weft is woven, each woven thread is referred to as a **pick**.

To begin, put the rigid heddle in the up position. Unwind enough yarn from the shuttle to extend about 3" (7.5 cm) beyond the width of the warp. Then pass the shuttle through the shed so that a tail of weft about 3" (7.5 cm) long hangs free beyond the selvedge. Pull the rigid heddle forward to align the weft perpendicular to the warp. You have now woven one pick. Place the rigid heddle in the down position. Tuck the free weft tail about 2" (5 cm) into the shed and allow it to exit out of the shed (you'll trim it later). Then unwind a bit more yarn from the shuttle and pass the shuttle through the shed in the opposite direction, placing the weft at about a 45-degree angle. Pull the rigid heddle forward to align this pick with the previous one. It is important to maintain an angle when laying the weft yarn in place. This angle will provide necessary extra length for the weft to travel over and under the individual warp threads.

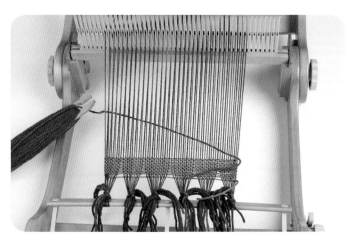

Pass the shuttle through the first shed, leaving a 3" (7.5 cm) tail at the selvedge edge.

Change sheds and tuck the weft tail into the new shed for about 2" (5 cm).

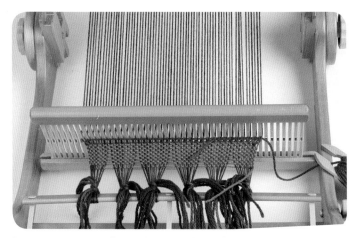

Pull the rigid heddle forward to align the weft picks.

Continue weaving by moving the heddle up or down, placing yarn in the shed, and beating it into place. It won't be long before the cloth grows and there isn't enough space for you to maintain the angle. At this point, you'll need to **advance the warp**. To advance the warp, release the tension from the back beam by pulling forward on the levers that release the back brake, then wind the woven cloth onto the front beam to make more space for the weft, being sure to stop winding when the fell line is still in front of the front beam. Place smooth paper between the first few revolutions of the cloth on the front beam, just as you did when winding the warp on the back beam. This will allow the cloth to wind onto the front beam evenly and decrease tension problems in the warp later. In most cases, it is not necessary to place paper between each layer, just the first few times the newly woven cloth winds around the cloth beam.

Selvedges

One of the hallmarks of beautiful cloth is straight edges or **selvedges**. Although the weft appears to follow a straight line from selvedge edge to selvedge edge, it actually follows a sinuous path as it bends over and under the individual warp threads. This is why we place the weft at an angle before we beat it into place—to allow for the extra length needed for this sinuous path. For balanced weaves, 45 degrees is about right; for warp-faced weaves (in which there are fewer warp ends to travel over and under), 20 degrees is about right. You'll want to experiment to determine what's best for each project (this is one reason why it's a good idea to allow for sampling when measuring the warp). If the angle is too small, the selvedges will draw in toward the center and crowd the warp threads; if it's too large, loops may form at the selvedges. Even experienced weavers can have trouble getting straight selvedges, so don't despair

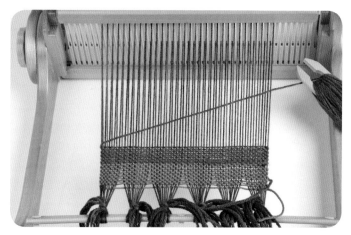

Place the weft in the shed at an angle to provide enough slack for a balanced weave.

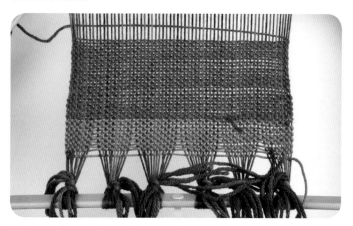

If there isn't enough slack in the weft, the selvedges will draw in.

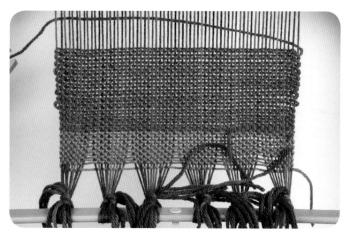

If there is too much slack in the weft, loops may form at the selvedges.

if yours aren't perfect. Like all acquired skills, it takes practice. Don't get too concerned about doing anything exactly "right;" as long as you do anything consistently, it will appear intentional!

Find Your Beat

Another key to beautiful cloth is consistent spaces between individual weft picks. The spacing between the warp ends is made uniform when the warp is threaded through the reed. Once a loom is warped, you don't have to worry about them. But the spacing between individual weft picks depends on how firmly you beat each pick with the rigid heddle, and that can vary a lot. Consider the photo below. The first inch was woven with a firm beat that packed the weft picks close to one another. In this section, there are more weft picks per inch than warp ends. The second inch was woven with a light beat that allowed considerable space between individual picks. In this section, there are fewer weft picks per inch than warp ends. The third inch was woven with an intermediate beat that produced the same number of weft picks per inch as warp ends. This section is woven with a balanced beat.

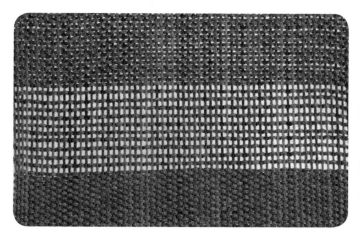

From bottom to top, this warp was woven with a firm beat, a light beat, and a balanced beat.

Depending on the look you want for your cloth, you may choose a firm, light, or balanced beat. All are fine. But whichever you choose, you want to be consistent throughout the entire project. This isn't as hard as it sounds—you'll quickly settle into a rhythm of forming the shed, passing the shuttle, and beating the weft, and this rhythm will result in uniform cloth. It's this rhythm that draws people to weaving.

Join New Weft

If you run out of yarn on your shuttle or the weft breaks, there is a simple method to start a new weft. Open a new shed and place the tail of the old weft into the new shed at an angle, allowing it to exit the warp. Bring the new yarn into the shed until it overlaps the old yarn, then exit its tail a few inches from the exiting tail of the old yarn and beat. Continue weaving.

measuring your progress

Once the cloth is rolled on the cloth beam it can be hard to tell how much cloth you have woven. A simple way to keep track is to measure the cloth as you weave. Before the cloth begins to wind on the cloth beam, use a tape measure to measure the amount that you've woven (be sure to begin your measurement where the warp is spread to its full width). Write down this number. Mark one selvedge with a contrasting thread and make a note of this measurement. Continue to weave until this marker thread reaches the front beam, then mark the selvedge with another contrasting thread. Add up the distances between marker threads to the first measurement and continue working in this manner.

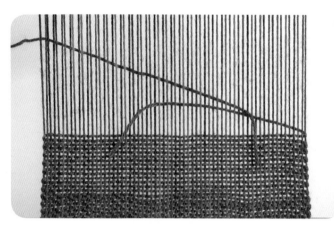

To join new weft yarn, overlap the old and new yarns for about 2" (5 cm), allowing tails of each to exit the warp.

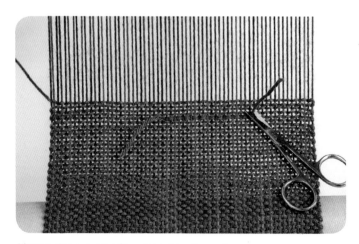

After you've woven a few picks, trim the ends.

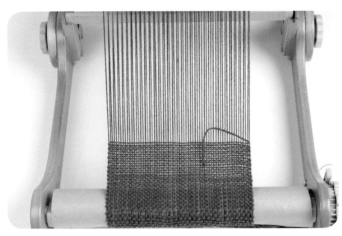

Place the end of the old weft at an angle in the next shed, leaving a tail on top.

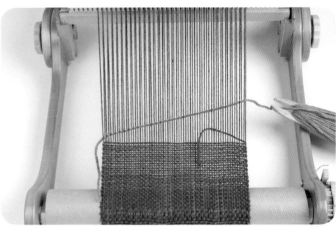

Bring the new yarn into the shed from the other side, leaving a tail at the selvedge.

Tuck the weft tail in the same shed as the second pick and beat them together.

Add New Color

To add a new color, start by cutting the yarn you have been working leaving a generous tail. Open a new shed and place the tail back into the shed bringing it up above the warp a couple of inches from the selvedge, leaving it at an angle. Starting from the opposite side of where you ended the old color, place the new color in the same shed, also at an angle and leaving a tail of this color hanging out from the edge.

Beat the yarns, then change the shed. Bring the new color tail back into the weft at an angle. Lay in a second pick of the new color, then beat it into place. Continue weaving as usual with the new yarn. Leave the tails until you've wet-finished the cloth.

weaving with two shuttles

When weaving two picks of the same color be sure to trap the nonworking weft at the selvedge.

When weaving more than two picks of each color, place the nonworking shuttle behind the rigid heddle and let the nonworking yarn act as the selvedge.

When weaving with two shuttles, it's important that you're consistent with how you manipulate the two yarns at the selvedges. For example, let's say you want to weave narrow two-pick stripes of red and brown for the Grab It and Go Bag on page 84. Begin by winding each color on a separate shuttle. Weave two picks of red in the usual manner, then place the shuttle within easy reach. Beginning from the same side that the red started, weave two picks with brown and place that shuttle within easy reach. Pick up the red shuttle so that the red yarn comes from under the brown, then weave two picks with red. Continue in this manner, always picking up new color from under the old. You may find that the selvedges aren't perfectly straight, but as long as you are consistent in how the yarns cross at the edges, you'll create a decorative repeating pattern on the selvedges.

This method works well if you're working just two picks. If you're working more than two picks, you'll want to allow the nonworking yarn to act like the selvedges. For example, in this plaid, I worked the first two picks as I did in the Grab and Go Bag, but for the other picks, I placed the shuttle behind the rigid heddle on the warp and allowed that yarn to follow the path of the selvedge. Then with my working weft, I catch both the selvedge and the nonworking weft.

THE END'S IN SIGHT

To finish, work a few picks with scrap yarn to hold the last picks of the cloth in place. Untie the warp from the front and back beams and pull the cloth off of the loom. If you don't plan to use any of the loom waste for fringe (or if you leave enough length for fringe before you cut), you can cut the warp near the apron rods instead of untying it. Be careful not to cut your apron cords! Remove the waste yarn from the loom. These waste yarns are called **thrums**. Some weavers save them to be used in other projects such a rug hooking, pom-poms, or for decorative elements such as rya knots or fringe.

Examine your cloth for any skips and fix them if necessary (see page 50). Trim all your joins to about 2" (5 cm) so they don't tangle in the wash, but leave tails long enough that if the yarn shrinks, the tails won't recede into the cloth and leave a gap.

Finishing Techniques

You have a few choices for finishing your weaving. Most of the projects in this book are finished with knotted or twisted fringe or with hemstitching, followed by fulling or gentle washing.

Hemstitching is worked with a needle and weft yarn while the project is still on the loom (see page 120). It holds the weft in place and creates a tidy edge for fringe. To finish cloth that has been hemstitched, simply remove the scrap yarn from the header (scrap yarn is not necessary at the final edge of cloth that has been hemstitched).

If you want a **knotted or twisted fringe**, trim the warp ends a few inches longer than the desired fringe length to keep the ends manageable. Place the cloth near the edge of a table so that a short end hangs off the edge. Place a book or other weight on top of the cloth to prevent it from slipping. Sit on a short stool or the floor so that the working ends are at eye level. Remove the scrap yarn at the end of the cloth and knot or twist the fringe as desired (see page 121). Repeat for the other end of the cloth.

If you want to create a dense, sturdy cloth, **full** it by subjecting it to water, soap, and agitation (see page 55). Fulling isn't an exact science, so it's important to monitor the progress. Because fulling involves shrinkage of the fibers, there's no going back to "unfull" an "overfulled" cloth.

Most handwovens should be washed by hand. To do this, fill a basin or tub with lukewarm water and add about a teaspoon of delicate soap and fabric softener, if desired. Gently move the fabric back and forth in the water a few times with your hands, being careful not to agitate so much that fulling occurs. Allow the fabric to soak for twenty minutes. Remove the cloth from the water, drain the water, refill the basin with clean room-temprature water, and return the cloth to rinse it. Repeat the rinse process as many times as necessary to remove all the soap from the cloth. Gently squeeze out the water, then roll the cloth in a clean towel to remove excess moisture. Lay it flat to dry.

Once the cloth is dry, use scissors or a rotary cutter against a self-healing mat to trim the fringe straight and to the desired length, then trim all tails flush with the cloth.

Untie knots.

Pull loose ends through rigid heddle and cut out waste yarn.

Tie the end into overhand knots.

All ends tied.

weaving mistakes

The most important thing to know about weaving mistakes is that not one is insurmountable. I have wound short warps, hacked color order, and had more tension problems than a Wall Street broker on a bad day. I have, however, never lost the battle. Sometimes it takes me longer to do a task than I thought it would, but everything is fixable (or the fabric turns into something other than originally envisioned). The most important lesson I've learned is that if things are going wrong, it's sometimes best to walk away. A good night's sleep can completely change my perspective. The second most important thing I've learned is that it is better to fix small mistakes as soon as they crop up so they don't become big problems later.

PROBLEM SOLVING

The three problems you're most likely to encounter are broken warp threads, weft floats or skips, and tension problems.

Broken Warp Threads

A broken warp end doesn't ruin a project. If a warp end breaks, simply pull that end free from the rigid heddle and replace it with a new piece of yarn. You'll need a T-pin and a small weight. I like to use a canister, jar, or small tin filled with dried beans or other similar objects for weight; S-hooks also work well. To start, place the T-pin into the woven cloth a few picks away from the fell line and so that the head is even with the gap left by the broken warp thread. Cut a new piece of warp about 18" (45.5 cm) longer than the length of the warp you think you have left to weave. Wrap one end of the new warp around the head of the T-pin. Thread the other end of the new warp through the vacant slot or hole in the rigid heddle to the back of the loom. Roll the end of the warp into a ball, place the ball in the container, and secure the lid so that the container hangs over the back beam and dangles in the air. Add weight to the container if there's not enough tension on the new warp end. You may want to weave a few picks before doing so. Continue weaving as usual for a few inches to secure the new warp. Remove the T-pin and needle weave (see page 120) the old and new warp ends into the fabric.

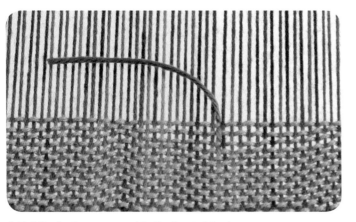

1. Pull the broken warp end to the front of the loom.

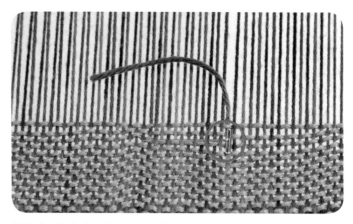

2. Tuck a T-pin into the woven cloth so that the head is even with the gap left by the broken warp thread.

3. Wrap one end of the new warp around the head of a T-pin.

4. Secure the new warp in a weighted canister or jar and let it hang off the back of the loom.

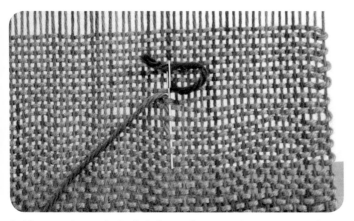

5. After weaving an inch of cloth, needle weave the new warp tail down the cloth.

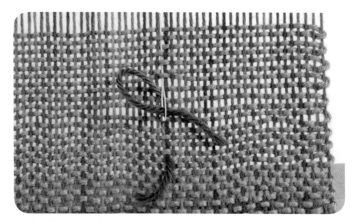

6. Needle weave the old warp tail up the cloth.

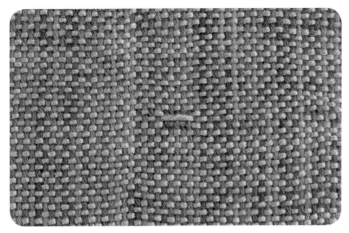

Floats occur when the weft doesn't travel over and under the warp properly.

To fix a float, thread a piece of weft yarn on a tapestry needle and needle weave the yarn along the correct path.

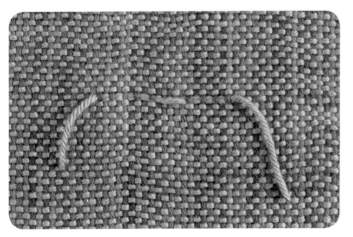

After washing the fabric, trim the ends of the replacement weft and cut the original weft at each end of the float.

The correction is barely visible in the finished cloth.

Weft Floats

Once the cloth is off the loom, take a good look at each side of the cloth to check for warp or weft skips or **floats**. Floats occur when a weft pick doesn't travel over and under the warp ends properly. They are generally caused when adjacent warp threads stick together so that a thread that was supposed to be raised doesn't go up or a thread that was supposed to be lowered doesn't go down. Get in the habit of checking for "clean" sheds to ensure against this and pay attention to the cloth as you weave. It's much easier to "unweave" a few picks to correct a float than to fix it after the cloth is off the loom.

If you do find a float after the cloth is off the loom, you can fix it with a bit of weft yarn threaded on a tapestry needle. Beginning and ending about an inch from the float, needle weave the yarn along the correct path. Wash the fabric to set the yarn. Trim the tails of the new weft, then cut the old weft at the float and trim those tails.

Tension Problems

Hopefully you can catch tension problems right away and fix them before they become a nuisance. If you've tied the warp to the apron rods with uneven tension across the width of the warp, the first few weft picks will appear wavy. The most common scenario is that one of the bundles of warp isn't tight enough. To fix this problem, simply unweave the first few picks and adjust the loose grouping. If the problem seems to be in more than one grouping, you may want to retie the entire warp.

Sometimes the problem is that the warp wasn't wound evenly on the back beam, which causes individual warp ends to loosen. To tighten these ends (or groups of ends), cut a piece of scrap yarn about 12" (30.5 cm) long, loop it around the loose thread(s) at the back beam, and secure the tails of the waste yarn in a weighted canister as used for fixing broken warp ends.

The weft will follow a wavy path if the warp is under uneven tension.

fully loaded **scarf**

a perfect first project, this scarf is finished by being thrown into the washing machine, which masks any irregularities in the weaving such as messy edges or uneven beating. A hand-cut edging gives a fun finished look. This fabric can be used for all sorts of projects since it can be cut without the possibility of fraying edges. Widen the warp to create a cloth large enough to cut out pieces for a simply shaped vest or hat. Keep in mind that about 30% of width and length will be lost during the fulling process.

Finished Dimensions
About 4½" (11.5 cm) wide by 57½" (146 cm) long, plus 2" (5 cm) fringe at each end.

Weave Structure
Balanced plain weave.

Equipment
10-dent rigid heddle with 7" (18 cm) weaving width; one stick shuttle.

Warp and Weft Specifications

Sett (epi)
10.

Weaving Width
6¾" (17 cm).

Picks per Inch (ppi)
10.

Warp Length
130" (330 cm; includes 30" [76 cm] for loom waste and take-up, and 10" [25.5 cm] for sampling).

Number of Warp Ends
66.

Warp Color Order
Alternate 2 lime green with 2 purple variegated, end with 2 lime green.

Yarns

Warp
2-ply sportweight wool (1,700 yd [1,554.5 m]/lb): 126 yd (115 m) lime green. 3-ply worsted-weight wool (1,000 yd [914.5 m]/lb): 115 yd (105 m) purple variegated.
Shown here: Brown Sheep Nature Spun Sport Weight (100% wool; 184 yd [168 m]/50 g): #144 Limestone (lime green). Universal Yarns Inc. Deluxe Worsted Magic: #903 purple variegated (100% wool; 1,006 yd [920 yd]/lb): #903 purple variegated.

Weft
2-ply sportweight wool (1,700 yd [1,554.5 m]/lb): 200 yd (183 m) forest green (includes yardage for sampling).
Shown here: Brown Sheep Nature Spun Sport Weight (100% wool; 184 yd [168 m]/50 g): #25 Enchanted Forest.

WARPING
Warp the loom (see page 24), following the specifications on page 53.

WEAVING
Weave a few inches of header to spread the warp ends (see page 40).

Weave with the forest green for at least 5" (12.5 cm) for a sample (you may try other colors of wool of the same brand) to test shrinkage later. Wools tend to shrink differently, and you will use this sample to test the amount of washing it will take to get the degree of fulling that you want—once the cloth is fulled there is no going back! Leave 3" (7.5 cm) of unwoven warp between the end of the sample and the beginning of the scarf. Weave 90" (229 cm) with forest green.

FINISHING
Remove the fabric from the loom (see page 46) by untying the warp from the apron rods. Remove the scrap yarn in the header. With sharp scissors, cut the sample section from the scarf.

Fulling
Full (see box at right) the sample to the desired thickness, then full the scarf to match (expect about 30% to be lost in width and length). Allow the fabric to thoroughly air-dry. Trim the loose threads from each end of the scarf.

Fringe
Using sharp scissors, cut fifteen slits at each end of the scarf, each about 2" (5 cm) long and about ¼" (6 mm) apart to form fringe.

the full story

The terms "fulling" and "felting" are often used interchangeably, although they refer to slightly different techniques. Felting is the process of agitating unspun protein fibers, such as wool, with needles or water to fuse the fibers together into a solid fabric. Fulling is the same process as felting—permanently interlocking microscopic barbs on protein fibers with agitation—but it is applied to wool yarn that has already been woven, knitted, or crocheted.

Fulling typically results in a fabric with more drape, while felting produces a sturdier, denser fabric. However, heavily fulled cloth can become very dense and felt-like, often resulting in fabric that can be cut without fraying. Either one causes the fabric to shrink both in width and length. The amount of shrinkage will vary with the yarn, water temperature, and amount of agitation.

Try combining yarns that full (wool and alpaca, for example) with yarns that don't (cotton, linen, rayon, and synthetics, for example). Called "differential shrinkage," this can cause wonderful bumps and textures in woven fabric.

Fulling Woven Fabric

You can full fabric by hand, but it takes a long time! It's much easier to use a washing machine if you monitor the process carefully. If your machine doesn't have an agitator, add a dense, heavy object such as a washable shoe to create agitation. Because all washing machines are a little different, you'll want to use a sample to test the amount of shrinkage before you full your entire project. Measure your sample before and after it goes through the washing machine to determine how much length and width will be lost by fulling.

For a lightly fulled fabric, set the machine on the delicate cycle (which has limited agitation) and warm water on a low water level. Let the machine fill with water, then add a couple of teaspoons of delicate washing soap along with the sample. Let the agitator run for a minute, then check the cloth to see how much fulling has occurred. If you're satisfied with the degree of fulling, remove the fabric from the machine, otherwise let it continue to agitate, checking the progress every minute or so. If the desired amount of fulling occurs before the rinse cycle begins, gently hand-rinse the fabric to remove the soap without causing further felting. Roll the sample in a towel to remove excess moisture, then lay it flat.

Decide if your sample fulled more or less than you want in the finished project. If you want your project to be less fulled, remove it from the washing machine sooner. If you want it more fulled, let it agitate longer. While it's possible to repeat the process to make the fabric denser, there's no going back to undo fulling that has already occurred.

You can also full your fabric by hand. Simply fill a basin (or your bathtub if your project is large) with lukewarm water. Add soap and the fabric, then agitate the project vigorously with your hands until you have the level of fullness you desire. This can take anywhere from a few minutes to upward of an hour! Rinse the fabric to rid it of any soap, then roll it in a towel to remove water, and lay it flat to air-dry.

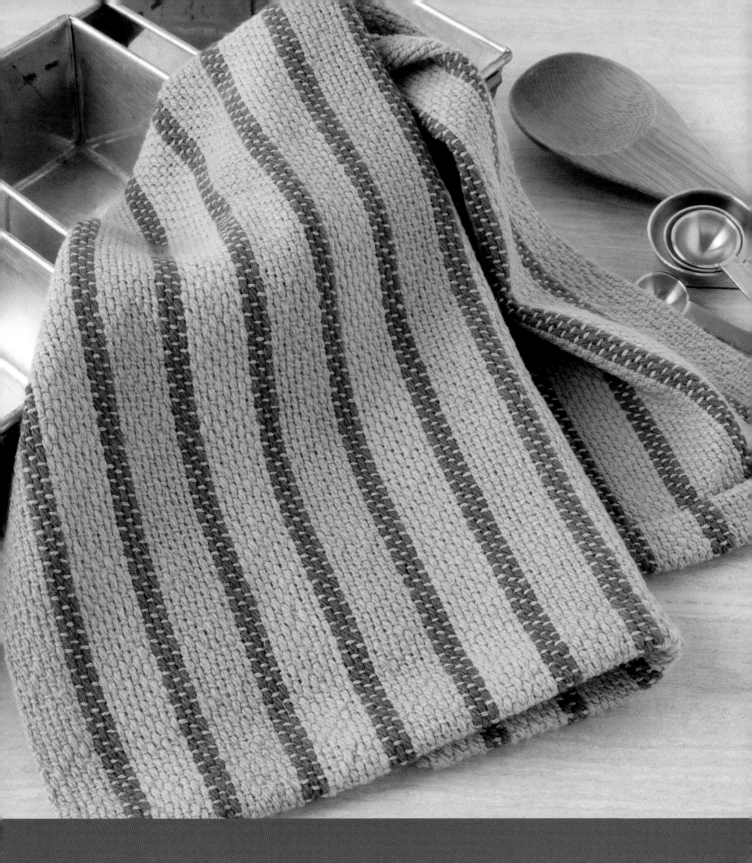

dealer's choice
placemats and towels

the same style of cloth can be good for more than one project. This fabric works equally well for placemats and towels—the choice is yours! Warping with worsted-weight cotton and weaving with a fine cotton weft allows the warp stripes to dominate and provides the towels with nice drape.

Finished Dimensions
Two Towels, each about 11¾" (30 cm) wide by 23" (58.5 cm) long.
or
Two Placemats, each about 11¾" (30 cm) wide by 19" (48.5 cm) long.

Weave Structure
Warp-dominant plain weave.

Equipment
8-dent rigid heddle with 15" (38 cm) weaving width; two stick shuttles.

Notions
Large-eyed sewing needle; Fray Check.

Warp and Weft Specifications

Sett (epi)
8.

Weaving Width
14¾" (37.5 cm).

Picks per Inch (ppi)
9.

Warp Length
88" (223.5 cm; includes 18" [45.5 cm] loom waste and take-up for towels and 27" [68.5 cm] for placemats).

Number of Warp Ends
118.

Warp Color Order
[8 blue, 3 purple, 8 turquoise, 3 purple] 5 times, 8 blue.

Yarns

Warp
4-ply worsted-weight cotton (792 yd [724 m]/lb): 130 yd (119 m) blue, 82 yd (75 m) purple, and 98 yd (90 m) turquoise.
Shown here: Lion Brand Yarns Kitchen Cotton (100% cotton; 99 yd [91 m]/2 oz): #108 Dusty Sky Blue (blue), #147 Grape (purple), and #148 Tropical Breeze (turquoise).

Weft
8/2 unmercerized cotton (3,369 yd [3,081 m]/lb): 233 yd (213 cm) turquoise for placemats; 273 yd (250 m) gray-blue for towels.
Shown here: Cotton Clouds Aurora Earth (100% cotton; 3,369 yd [3,081 m]/lb): #56 Light Turk (turquoise) and #47 Copen (gray-blue).

WARPING

Warp the loom (see page 24), following the specifications on page 57.

WEAVING

Wind one of the stick shuttles with a generous amount of scrap yarn.

Wind the second stick shuttle with turquoise for placemats or with gray-blue for towels.

Weave a few inches of header to spread the warp ends (see page 40).

Placemats

Weave 26" (66 cm) with turquoise for the first placemat, 2" (5 cm) with scrap yarn to keep the weft in place when the placemats are cut apart and to provide a firm foundation for the second placemat. Weave another 26" (66 cm) with turquoise for the second placement, then 1" (2.5 cm) with scrap yarn.

Towels

Weave 30½" (77.5 cm) with gray-blue for the first towel, then 2" (5 cm) with scrap yarn to keep the weft in place when the towels are cut apart and to provide a firm foundation for the second towel. Weave another 30½" (77.5 cm) with gray-blue for the second towel, then 1" (2.5 cm) with scrap yarn.

Note: The different-colored wefts emphasize either the turquoise or the gray-blue warp stripes. The effect is subtle. You can choose which one you like.

FINISHING

Remove the fabric from the loom (see page 46). Apply Fray Check along each end of each placemat or towel and allow to dry thoroughly. Cut the placemats or towels apart in the center of the scrap yarn bands. Remove the scrap yarn. Machine wash the placemats or towels on the gentle cycle with mild soap and tumble dry on the low setting. Remove from the dryer while still damp, then press until fully dry.

Trim the fringe to ¼" (6 mm) using a rotary cutter on a self-healing mat.

Fold each cut end over ¼" (6 mm), then fold over again ½" (1.3 cm) and pin in place. With the weft yarn threaded on a large-eyed sewing needle, whipstitch the fold in place.

bobbled slippers

shrinking fabric on purpose provides endless opportunities for making shaped garments, bags, belts, and even shoes! If you combine yarns that shrink with yarns that don't in the warp and weft, your fabric will be covered in bumps. If you combine these yarns in the warp and use only a yarn that shrinks in the weft, you'll produce a fabric with long wavy stripes. Experiment to see what other effects you can produce.

Finished Dimensions
About 10" (25.5 cm) long; to fit a woman's foot.

Weave Structure
Plain weave with differential shrinkage.

Equipment
10-dent rigid heddle with 14" (35.5 cm) weaving width; two stick shuttles.

Warp and Weft Specifications
Sett (epi)
10.

Weaving Width
14" (35.5 cm).

Picks per Inch (ppi)
8.

Warp Length
100" (254 cm; includes 30" [76 cm] for loom waste and take-up).

Number of Warp Ends
141 doubled ends.

Warp and Weft Color Order
Warp: Using two threads together as one, alternate 3 yellow and 3 blue green, ending with 3 yellow.
Weft: Using two threads together as one, alternate 3 yellow and 3 mint green, ending with 3 yellow.

Yarns

Warp
2-ply 2/8 fingering-weight wool (2,240 yd [2,048 m]/lb): 400 yd (366 m) yellow.
2-ply 10/2 laceweight mercerized cotton (4,000 yd [3,352 m]/lb): 385 yd (352 m) blue-green.
Shown here: Jaggerspun Main Line 2/8 (100% wool) in Daffodil (yellow).
Lunatic Fringe 10/2 mercerized cotton (100% cotton) in Blue Green.

Weft
2-ply 2/8 fingering-weight wool (2,240 yd [2,048 m]/lb): 240 yd (219 m) yellow.
2-ply laceweight mercerized cotton (4,000 yd [3,352 m] lb): 239 yd (218.5 m) mint green.
Shown here: Jaggerspun Main Line 2/8 (100% wool) in Daffodil (yellow).
UKI 10/2 mercerized cotton (100% cotton) in Willow Green (mint green).

Trim
2-ply 3/8 sportweight wool (1,490 yd [1,362.5 m]/lb): 5 yd [4.5 m] green.
Shown here: Jaggerspun Main Line 3/8 (100% wool) in Capri Green.

WARPING

Measure the Warp

Because the warp is wound in pairs, it will help to use yarn wound on mini cones. Place two cones of yellow in a cone holder or in two tall, narrow containers. Wind the warp (see page 34) using two strands as one, placing a finger between the two to keep them from tangling. Wind seventy-two double-stranded ends. Tie a choke.

Place two blue-green cones in the holder or containers and wind sixty-nine doubled-stranded ends of blue-green in the same manner. Tie a choke.

Wind the Shuttle

Place two cones of yellow in a cone holder or container and wind a shuttle with double strands of yellow. Wind another shuttle with double strands of mint green.

Thread the Reed

Warp the loom (see page 24), following the specifications on page 61, threading *three yellow double-ends, then skipping three spaces; repeat from * for the entire 14" (35.5 cm) width. Thread the blue-green double-ends in the empty spaces. Check your work—it is easier to correct threading errors before the warp is wound onto the back beam.

WEAVING

Weave a few picks of cotton scrap yarn (cotton will be easy to remove) to spread the warp ends (see page 40). Using a loose beat, weave three picks with yellow. Add green and weave three picks with green. Alternate three picks each of yellow and green for the entire length of the warp (see page 45 for tips on working with two shuttles). Don't worry too much about maintaining even selvedges—they won't be seen in the final project.

FINISHING

Remove the fabric from the loom (see page 46). Remove the scrap yarn in the header.

Fulling

Full (see page 55) the entire length of the fabric in the washing machine set for a normal cycle with enough warm water to allow complete submersion. Check the fabric periodically for progress—you want it to shrink to about 5½" (14 cm) wide or until "bobbles" begin to appear. Reset the washer if necessary to get the desired amount of shrinkage. Remove the fabric from the washer and rinse it thoroughly, then roll it in a towel to squeeze out the excess moisture and lay it flat to air-dry.

Assembly

Photocopy the pattern pieces at right on stiff card stock, enlarging as necessary so that each square equals 1" (2.4 cm). Cut the pieces out and pin them to the fabric. Cut the dry fabric, using the templates as a guide. Using yellow and an overhand stitch, sew one top flap to one sole, with the arch facing to the left, then sew the other top flap to the other sole, with the arch pointing to the right. Sew one back piece to each sole and front flap. Fold the extra fabric from the back piece so that it is even with the front flap and stay-stitch it in place by taking one stitch on each side. Using the green sportweight wool, sew decorative blanket stitches around the sole of each slipper.

Gently handwash the slippers in warm water using mild soap and rubbing the stitching to full it ever so slightly. Roll the slippers in a towel, then shape as desired (place a small cloth or tissue paper in the toes) and allow to air-dry completely.

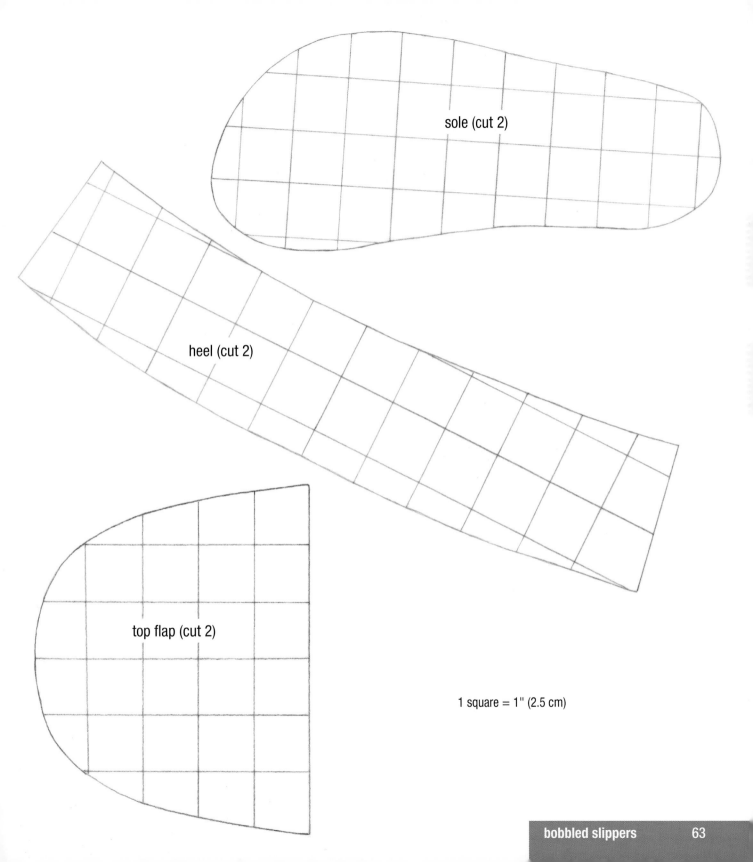

sole (cut 2)

heel (cut 2)

top flap (cut 2)

1 square = 1" (2.5 cm)

color-play plaid

plaid provides endless opportunities to play with color. This scarf uses two purples close in hue to provide subtle color play that stands in contrast to an analogous blue with a brighter value. Now if this sentence sounds like gobbledegook, it's because the terms "value," "hue," and "analogous" are words we used to describe color (see Color in Weaving, page 19). Said another way: Pick two similar purples and add a bright blue and see what happens! This scarf uses another nifty trick—a whipstitch is worked along each selvedge edge as the cloth is woven to visually balance the colors while masking potentially messy selvedges.

Finished Dimensions
About 8¼" (21 cm) wide by 53½" (136 cm) long, plus 2" (5 cm) fringe at each end.

Weave Structure
Plain weave.

Equipment
10-dent rigid heddle with 9" (23 cm) weaving width; three stick shuttles; tapestry needle.

Warp and Weft Specifications
Sett (epi)
10.
Weaving Width
9" (23 cm).
Picks per Inch (ppi)
6.

Warp Length
100" (256 cm; includes 30" [76 cm] for loom waste and take-up, and 10" [25.5 cm] for sampling).

Number of Warp Ends
90.

Warp Color Order
10 dark purple, 10 light purple, 10 ice blue, 10 light purple, 10 dark purple, 10 light purple, 10 ice blue, 10 light purple, 10 dark purple.

Weft Color Order
8 dark purple [6 light purple, 6 ice blue, 6 light purple, 6 dark purple] 15 times, end 8 dark purple.

Yarns

Warp
Bulky singles in a wool/mohair/cashmere blend (1,097 yd [1,003 m]/lb): 85 yd (77.5 m) dark purple, 115 yd (105 m) light purple, and 60 yd (55 m) ice blue.
Shown here: Harrisville Designs Orchid Yarns (70% fine wool, 25% mohair, 5% cashmere; 184 yd [168 m]/100 g): #255 Amethyst (dark purple), #256 Wisteria (light purple), and #257 Tibetan Blue (ice blue).

Weft
Bulky singles in a wool/mohair/cashmere blend (1,097 yd [1,003 m]/lb): 27 yd (24.5 m) dark purple, 50 yd (45.5 m) light purple, and 30 yd (27.5 m) ice blue (7 yd [6.5 m] included here for whipstitching selvedges and hemstitching ends). Additional yarn will be needed for sampling.
Shown here: Harrisville Designs Orchid Yarns (70% fine wool, 25% mohair, 5% cashmere; 1,097 yd [1,003 m]/lb): #255 Amethyst (dark purple), #256 Wisteria (light purple), and #257 Tibetan Blue (ice blue).
Note: This yarn has been discontinued. Substitute Brown Sheep Lamb's Pride Worsted (85% wool, 15% mohair; 190 yd [173 m]/113 g).

PROJECT NOTES

Weaving Plaid

Plaids require a lot of color changes (see page 44). Because there are an odd number of picks in each weft stripe, each stripe will end on the opposite side from where it started. When starting a new weft, be sure to start on the opposite side of the previous tucked tail to evenly distribute the extra bulk caused by the tucked tails.

Selvedge Treatment

To mask messy selvedges and visually balance the colors in the plaid, use ice blue threaded on a tapestry needle to whipstitch (see page 121) along each selvedge. For simplicity, thread 3 yards of ice blue on each of two tapestry needles. Using one needle at each selvedge, stop to work whipstitches along the edges after every few inches of cloth have been woven.

WARPING

Wind each color of warp separately.

Warp the loom (see page 24), following the specifications on page 65.

WEAVING

Weave an inch or two of header to spread the warp ends (see page 40).

Weave a sample to determine the degree of fulling you want. Leave 4" (10 cm) of unwoven warp between the sample and the beginning of the scarf.

Leave a 5" (12.5 cm) weft tail at the selvedge, then using a soft beat, weave one pick. Change sheds, tuck the 5" (12.5 cm) tail into the shed, allowing 1" (2.5 cm) to poke out. Weave another pick in the same shed and beat. Continue weaving a few inches with weft yarn according to the weft color order on page 65, adding whipstitches of ice blue along each selvedge (going around one warp and two wefts) as you go. Thread 25" (63.5 cm) of ice blue on a tapestry needle and use it to hemstitch (see page 120) around two warps and two wefts at the starting end of the scarf. Continue to weave and add whipstitches along the selvedges until the scarf measures 61" (155 cm; to produce a finished length of about 53" [134.5 cm]), ending at the right selvedge. Cut the weft, leaving an 6" (15 cm) tail. Needle weave (see page 120) this end back into the cloth. Thread 25" (63.5 cm) of ice blue on a tapestry needle and use it to hemstitch as before.

FINISHING

Remove the fabric from the loom (see page 46). Remove the scrap yarn in the header. With sharp scissors, cut the sample section from the fabric.

Fulling

Full (see page 55) the sample to the desired thickness, then full the scarf to match. Allow the fabric to thoroughly air-dry.

Trim the fringe to 2" (5 cm) using a rotary cutter on a self-healing mat.

two-skein scarf

the trick to weaving with variegated yarns is to use them in such a way as to bring out their beauty without combining too many colors so that they end up looking muddy. One trick is to grab a skein of beautifully variegated yarn and find a coordinating solid that will complement the variegated colorway, as in this scarf of subtle beauty. Simple hemstitching allows the variegated yarn to show in the fringe. For a different look, use the solid color in the warp and weave with the variegated.

Finished Dimensions
About 9" (23 cm) wide by 58½" (148.5 cm) long, plus 6" (15 cm) fringe at each end.

Weave Structure
Plain weave.

Equipment
10-dent rigid heddle with 10" (25.5 cm) weaving width; one stick shuttle.

Warp and Weft Specifications

Sett (epi)
10.

Weaving Width
10" (25.5 cm).

Picks per Inch (ppi)
8.

Warp Length
90" (229 cm; includes 20" [51 cm] for loom waste and take-up; this does not allow for sampling).

Number of Warp Ends
100.

Yarns

Warp
4-ply wool/silk blend (1,150 yd [1,051.5 m]/lb): 250 yd (228.5 m) variegated.

Shown here: Mountain Colors Twizzle (85% merino, 15% silk; 1,142 yd [1,044 m]/lb): Indian Corn.

Weft
2-ply alpaca/wool/metallic blend (1,250 yd [1,143 m] lb): 135 yd teal.

Shown here: Nashua Handknits Ivy (50% alpaca, 45% merino, 5% estellina; 1,252 yd [1,145 m]/lb): Blue Teal.

Note: This yarn has been discontinued. Substitute Cascade Hollywood (87% superwash wool, 10% acrylic, 3% polyester; 208 yd [190 m]/100 g).

WARPING

Warp the loom (see page 24), following the specifications on page 69.

WEAVING

Weave an inch or two of header to spread the warp ends (see page 40).

Leave a 30" (76 cm) weft tail at the selvedge to use for hemstitching later, then using a soft beat, weave a few inches with weft yarn. Thread the weft tail on a tapestry needle and use it to hemstitch (see page 120) around two warps and two wefts at the starting end of the scarf. Continue to weave until the scarf measures 60" (152.5 cm). Cut the weft, leaving a 30" (76 cm) tail. Thread the tail on a tapestry needle and use it to hemstitch as before.

FINISHING

Remove the fabric from the loom (see page 46), using the loom waste for fringe. Remove the scrap yarn in the header.

Handwash in lukewarm water with mild soap, rinse. Roll in a towel and squeeze out excess water. Lay flat to dry. Trim the fringe to 6" (15 cm) using a rotary cutter on a self-healing mat.

what is a variegated yarn?

I've seen the term "variegated" applied to yarns that are simply multicolored (for instance, two different colors plied together). "Variegated" refers to a yarn that has repeating bands of color along the length of the yarn. There are a bevy of beautiful handpainted variegated yarns on the market. When you weave with these yarns in the weft, "pooling" occurs if the bands of color stack upon one another. It is all too easy to lose the great colors when a variegated weft yarn interlaces with the warp yarn. Use the tips in the Two-Skein Scarf on page 69 and Piping Hot Pillows on page 73 to weave with these yarns for smashing results.

piping hot **pillows**

weaving with variegated yarns means that you can get lots of patterning and color with very little effort, if you pick your colors right. These two pillows show three ways to weave with variegated yarns—variegated as warp, variegated as weft, and variegated as warp and weft. The fabric is sewn into a square and stuffed with a commercial pillow form. The pillows are neatly finished with a loom-woven tubular weave band piping. You could also embellish the pillows by stitching on lengths of tubular weave in free-form designs.

Finished Dimensions
About 14" square.

Weave Structure
Plain weave.

Equipment
8-dent rigid heddle with 16" weaving width; one stick shuttle; tapestry needle.

Warp and Weft Specifications

Sett (epi)
8.

Weaving Width
Pillow—15½".
Piping—1¼".

Picks per Inch (ppi)
Pillow—6.
Piping—3.

Warp Length
Each Pillow—64" (162.5 cm; includes 30" [76 cm] for loom waste and take-up).
Each Piping—86" (218 cm; includes 30" [76 cm] for loom waste and take-up).

Number of Warp Ends
Pillow—124.
Piping—10.

Yarns

Pillow Warp
Single-spun heavy worsted-weight wool (630 yd [576 m]/lb): 221 yd (202 m) red or variegated.
Shown here: Manos del Uruguay (100% wool; 630 yd [576 m]/lb): #69 red or #113 Wildflower.

Pillow Weft
Single-spun heavy worsted-weight wool (630 yd [576 m]/lb): 45 yd (41 m) each red and pastel variegated.
2-ply sportweight wool (1,700 yd [1,554.5 m]/lb): 16 yd (14.5 m) red (for hem only).
Shown here: Manos del Uruguay (100% wool; 630 yd [576 m]/lb): #69 red and #113 Wildflower.
Brown Sheep Nature Spun Sport Weight (100% wool; 1,700 yd [1,554.5 m]/lb): #44 Husker Red.

Piping Warp
Single-spun heavy worsted-weight wool (630 yd [576 m]/lb): 24 yd (22 m) red or pastel variegated.
Shown here: Manos del Uruguay (100% wool; 630 yd [576 m]/lb): #69 red or #113 Wildflower.

Piping Weft
Single-spun heavy worsted-weight wool (630 yd [576 m]/lb): 7 yd (6.5 m) red or pastel variegated.
Shown here: Manos del Uruguay (100% wool; 630 yd [576 m]/lb): #69 red or #113 Wildflower.

Other Supplies
Coordinating sewing thread and sharp-point sewing needle; 14" x 14" (35.5 x 35.5 cm) pillow form (form shown by Eco Craft (cotton fabric stuffed with corn fiber); Fray Check (available at fabric and craft stores).

PROJECT NOTES

Although the warp is a bulky single-spun yarn, it holds up remarkably well under tension and can withstand a fair amount of abrasion without fraying.

Because this fabric has more warp ends per inch than weft picks, whichever yarn is in the warp will appear more dominant.

WARPING

Using the red warp for one pillow and the pastel variegated warp for the other, warp the loom (see page 24), following the specifications on page 73.

Wind three stick shuttles: one with bulky red, one with bulky variegated, and one with fingering-weight wool.

WEAVING THE PILLOW

Weave an inch or two with scrap yarn to spread the warp ends (see page 40).

Leave a 30" (76 cm) tail to use for hemstitching later, then using a soft beat, weave 1" (2.5 cm) with fingering-weight wool. Thread the weft tail on a tapestry needle and use it to hemstitch (see page 120) around two warps and wefts at the starting end of the scarf. Weave 16" (40.5 cm) with the variegated yarn, then switch to red and weave another 16" (40.5 cm), and finish by weaving 1" (2.5 cm) with the fingering-weight wool. Cut the weft, leaving a 30" (76 cm) tail. Thread the tail on a tapestry needle and use it to hemstitch as before.

FINISHING

Remove the fabric from the loom (see page 46). Remove the scrap yarn in the header.

WEAVING THE PIPING

Weave one piping with red warp and one piping with variegated warp. The piping is woven separately in a structure called tubular weave. To weave tubular weave, warp the loom with ten 86" (218.5 cm) warp ends. Wind a short stick shuttle with 2½ yards (2.3 meters) of weft yarn. Leave a 6" (15 cm) weft tail at the right selvedge if you're right-handed or at the left selvedge if you're left-handed, to use to cinch the end, then pass the shuttle through the shed. Change the shed without bringing the reed to the fell of the cloth. Bring the shuttle under the warp and back to the same side where it entered the shed before. Pass the shuttle through the new shed. Holding the shuttle in your palm, pinch the exiting yarn between your thumb and index finger about 2" (5 cm) from the selvedge, tug firmly downward on the weft yarn to move it into place. Take care to not pinch the yarn too far from the shed and exert too much pressure, as singles yarn has a tendency to pull apart. Continue weaving in this manner for a few inches, always entering the shed from the same side so that the narrow warp forms a tube. Make several half-hitch knots with the weft to cinch the end of the piping. Continuing weaving until the tube measures 56" (142 cm) long (you will lose about 17% of the length due to take-up and shrinkage once it is washed).

FINISHING

Full (see page 55) the pillow and piping fabric in the washing machine set for a gentle cycle with mild soap and warm water or handwash the fabric using warm water and mild soap. If handwashing, gently agitate the cloth for a few minutes to encourage the fabric to full, then gently squeeze out the water by wrapping the fabric in a towel. With either method, lay the fabric flat to air-dry. Trim the fringe right up to the knot on the piping and the hemstitching on the pillow.

weaving tubular weave

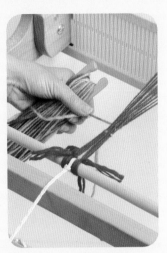

1. Pass the shuttle through the shed, leaving a 6" (15 cm) tail at the selvedge.

2. Change the shed and bring the shuttle under warp and around to same side it previously entered.

3. Pass the shuttle through the new shed, then tug downward on the weft to tighten the piping.

4. Tie the weft tail in the second half hitch to cinch the end of the piping.

Assembly

Fold the 1" (2.5 cm) of fabric woven with the fingering yarn to the wrong side of the pillow fabric and, using sewing thread, whipstitch (see page 121) it in place to form a hem. Repeat on the other end. Fold the cloth in half so that the seams are facing out. Using a tapestry needle and the thin weft, work a baseball stitch (see page 120) under the first thick pick to assure that the seam is hidden when sewn, then sew the two ends together. Sew one of the sides to form an envelope. Turn the fabric right side out and place the pillow form inside the fabric envelope. Fold the remaining open side down inside the pillow about 1" (2.5 cm) and sew the fabric together close to the edge of pillow form.

Place the knotted end of piping at the center of one side of the sewn pillow. Using coordinating sewing thread, use whipstitches to sew the base of the piping to the pillow seam. Sew the piping around all four sides. Cut the piping so that the end just covers the knot where you began, seal the cut with Fray Check, and sew the sealed end over the knot.

layered cravat

short decorative scarves tied snuggly at the nape of the neck provide an elegant touch to your day. Usually thought of as a man's accessory, this two-layered interpretation weaves up quickly and uses very little yarn, allowing you to freely use luxury yarns with smashing results. A blend of fine kid mohair was used in both the warp and weft on this cravat. Although mohair is a sticky yarn that can be tricky when used as a warp, the loose sett used here helps alleviate the problem. The yarns in the two layers shown here are close in hue, but one has a dash of metallic for a subtle sparkle.

Finished Dimensions
2 scarves, each about 6" (15 cm) wide by 33" (84 cm) long, plus 1" (2.5 cm) fringe at each end.

Weave Structure
Plain weave.

Equipment
10-dent rigid heddle with 6" (15 cm) weaving width; two stick shuttles.

Warp and Weft Specifications

Sett (epi)
10.

Weaving Width
6" (15 cm).

Picks per Inch (ppi)
8.

Warp Length
98" (249 cm; includes 30" [76 cm] for loom waste and take-up).

Number of Warp Ends
60.

Yarns

Warp
2-ply laceweight kid mohair/merino wool/microfiber blend (5,000 yd [4,572 m]/lb): 165 yd (151 m) light blue (#4681).
Shown here: Crystal Palace Kid Merino (28% kid mohair, 28% merino wool, 44% microfiber; 240 yd [219.5 m]/25 g): #4681 Misty Blue (light blue).

Weft
2-ply laceweight kid mohair/silk/polyester/nylon blend (4,700 yd [4,295.5 m]/lb): 49 yd (45 m) gray.
2-ply laceweight kid mohair/merino wool/microfiber blend (5,000 yd [4,572 m]/lb): 46 yd (42 m) light blue.
Shown here: Rowan Kidsilk Night (67% kid mohair, 18% silk, 10% polyester, 5% nylon; 227 yd [207.5 m]/25 g): #608 Moonlight (gray). *Note: This yarn has been discontinued. Substitute Rowan Kidsilk*

Haze Eclipse (66% mohair, 27% silk, 4% polyester, 3% nylon; 219 yd [200 m]/125 g). Crystal Palace Kid Merino (28% kid mohair, 28% merino wool, 44% microfiber; 240 yd [219.5 m]/25 g): #4681 Misty Blue (light blue).

WARPING

Wind each weft color separately on a stick shuttle.

Warp the loom (see page 24), following the specifications on page 77.

WEAVING

Weave under moderate tension so as not to break the fine threads and use a soft hand when beating in the weft shots. Weave an inch or two header to spread the warp ends (see page 40). Leaving a 30" (76 cm) tail to use for hemstitching later, with gray, weave 1" (2.5 cm). Thread the weft tail on a tapestry needle and use it to hemstitch (see page 120) around two warps and two wefts at the starting end of the scarf. Weave 34" (86.5 cm), ending at the right selvedge. Cut the weft, leaving a 30" (76 cm) tail. Thread the tail on a tapestry needle and use it to hemstitch as before.

Advance the warp so that there is a 4" (10 cm) gap from the end of the first scarf, then repeat the process with light blue for the second scarf.

FINISHING

Remove the fabric from the loom (see page 46), leaving at least 2" (5 cm) loom waste at each end for fringe. Remove the waste yarn from the header. With sharp scissors, cut the two scarf sections apart in the center of the 4" (10 cm) gap between the woven sections. Washing is not necessary. Trim the fringe on each end of each scarf to 1" (2.5 cm) with a rotary cutter against a self-healing mat.

tweed so fine

weaving fine fabrics on the rigid-heddle loom is simply a matter of doubling or tripling fine yarns to create beautiful basketweave fabric. This type of fabric practically spills off the loom. Basketweave is formed on the rigid-heddle loom when groups of two or more wefts weave under and over equal groups of two or more warps. In this scarf, three ends of a fingering-weight wool-silk yarn are used as a single warp end and weft pick. Using a combination of mossy colors creates a sophisticated tweedy look.

Finished Dimensions
About 5¼" (13.5 cm) wide by 64" (162.5 cm) long, plus 4½" (11.5 cm) fringe at each end.

Weave Structure
Basketweave.

Equipment
8-dent rigid heddle with 6" (15 cm) weaving width; one stick shuttle.

Warp and Weft Specifications

Sett (epi)
8.

Weaving Width
6" (15 cm).

Picks per Inch (ppi)
10.

Warp Length
100" (256 cm; includes 30" [76 cm] for loom waste and take-up; 9" [23 cm] of the loom waste is used for fringe).

Number of Warp Ends
48 (using three ends as one).

Yarns

Warp
2-ply fingering-weight wool/silk blend (5,040 yd [4,608.5 m]/lb): 134 yd (122.5 m) each of tan, forest green, and blue.
Shown here: Jaggerspun 2/18 Zephyr Wool/Silk (50% wool, 50% silk; 5,040 yd [4,608.5 m]): Suede (tan), Bottle Green (forest green), and Marine Blue (blue).

Weft
2/18 fingering-weight wool/silk blend (5,040 yd [4,608.5 m]/lb): 130 yd (119 m) each of tan, forest green, and blue.
Shown here: Jaggerspun 2/18 Zephyr Wool/Silk (50% wool, 50% silk; 5,040 yd [4,608.5 m]/lb): Suede (tan), Bottle Green (forest green), and Marine Blue (blue).

WARPING

Place each cone or ball of yarn in a container to keep the warp from tangling while winding the warp and stick shuttle. Use the three yarns together as one.

Warp the loom (see page 24) according to the specifications on page 81. The loom waste will be used for fringe, so be sure to allow 4½" (11.5 cm) of warp length when tying the warp onto the front apron rod.

WEAVING

Weave an inch or two with scrap yarn to spread the warp ends (see page 40). Leaving a 30" (76 cm) tail to use for hemstitching later, weave for 1" (2.5 cm). Thread the weft tail on a tapestry needle and use it to hemstitch (see page 120) around two warps and wefts at the starting end of the scarf. Weave 69" (175 cm) more, then cut the weft, leaving a 30" (76 cm) tail. Thread the tail on a tapestry needle and use it to hemstitch as before.

FINISHING

Remove the fabric from the loom (see page 46), leaving at least 4½" (11.5 cm) of loom waste at each end for fringe. Remove the scrap yarn in the header.

Handwash with delicate soap, then rinse. Roll the piece in a towel to remove excess moisture, then lay flat to dry. Trim fringe to 4" (10 cm) by hand or with a rotary cutter.

grab it and go **bag**

you'll find a million uses for this everyday bag. The simple design involves two strips of fabric—one for the body and the other for the handle—woven on the same warp. The houndstooth check is created through a simple color-and-weave technique (see page 87). The sturdy and inexpensive cotton yarn makes this a great project for gifts. Allow an additional 100" (254 cm) in warp length for each additional bag, but because there is a limit to the length of warp that can be wound onto the back beam, only plan for four bags at a time.

Finished Dimensions
About 10½" (26.5 cm) wide by 10¼" (26 cm) long, with 43" (109 cm) strap.

Weave Structure
Balanced plain weave with color-and-weave effect.

Equipment
8-dent rigid heddle with 7" (18 cm) weaving width; two stick shuttles.

Warp and Weft Specifications

Sett (epi)
8.

Weaving Width
6¾" (17 cm).

Picks per Inch (ppi)
8.

Warp Length
130" (includes 30" [76 cm] for loom waste and take-up).

Number of Warp Ends
54.

Warp Color Order
Alternate 2 ends of red and 2 ends of brown, end with 2 ends of red.

Weft Color Order
Alternate 2 picks of red and 2 picks of brown.

Yarns

Warp
4-ply bulky-weight unmercerized cotton (400 yd [366 m]/lb): 106 yd (97 m) red and 94 yd (86 m) brown.
Shown here: Peaches & Crème (100% cotton) in #96 Brick Red and #121 Chocolate.

Weft
4-ply bulky-weight unmercerized cotton (400 yd/lb): 80 yd (73 m) red and 80 yd (73 m) brown.
Shown here: Peaches & Crème (100% cotton) in #96 Brick Red and #121 Chocolate.

WARPING

Wind each color of warp separately.

Warp the loom (see page 24) according to the specifications on page 85, starting and ending with red warp ends.

Wind each color on a separate shuttle.

WEAVING

Weave an inch or two of header to spread the warp ends (see page 40).

Leaving a 24" (61 cm) tail at the selvedge to use for hemstitching later, weave two picks of red. Starting the brown from the same side as the red exited, but in a different shed, weave two picks of brown. Pick up the red shuttle from under the brown thread so that it catches neatly at the edge (see Managing Two Shuttles, page 45), and weave two picks with red. Do the same with the brown. Thread the red weft tail on a tapestry needle and use it to hemstitch (see page 120) around two warps and two wefts at the beginning of the piece.

Continue alternating two picks each of red and brown until the cloth measures 25" (63.5 cm); it doesn't matter which color you end with. Cut the weft, leaving a 24" (61 cm) tail. Thread the tail on a tapestry needle and use it to hemstitch as before. Cut the other weft yarn and needleweave (see page 120) the end back into the cloth.

Advance the warp, leaving 1" (2.5 cm) of unwoven warp. Weave a second section of cloth measuring 72" (183 cm) long, hemstitched at both ends as before.

FINISHING

Remove the fabric from the loom (see page 46). Remove the scrap yarn in the header. With sharp scissors, cut apart the two pieces. Machine wash with mild soap and allow to air-dry.

Trim the fringe ¼" (6 mm) from the hemstitching.

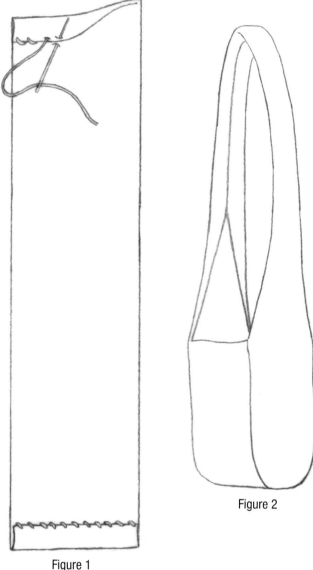

Figure 1

Figure 2

ASSEMBLY

Fold over each end of the shorter piece ¼" (6 mm) two times for hem, hiding the hemstitching. With red, use a whipstitch (see page 121) to sew the hem in place (Figure 1). Repeat for both sides of the longer fabric.

Fold the shorter body fabric in half widthwise with the hem facing inward. Fold the long piece of cloth for the strap. Align each end of the strap with the fold in the body cloth and tuck two picks (one strip of red) of the strap

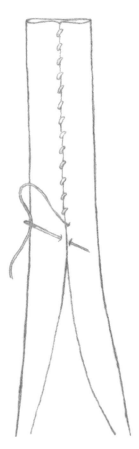

Figure 3

under the body fabric to form a seam allowance, making sure that the pattern is aligned across the entire fabric. With red, sew the two pieces together. Repeat for the other side, taking care not to twist the strap (Figure 2).

Using a whipstitch, sew the two selvedge edges of the strap together on the underside of the strap, beginning and ending 3" from the bag body. Allow the edges of the strap to taper to full width at the top of the bag and stitch in place (Figure 3).

To form a flat base, push the sewn ends of the strap into points, then fold the points so that they butt up against the side seams and stitch in place.

color and weave

Dozens of patterns can be created by clever combinations of light and dark yarns in the warp and weft. The patterns show up best if there is high contrast between the light and dark yarns. Color with low contrast will create interesting effects, but they won't be as sharply defined.

In the sampler shown here, two ends of purples are alternated with two ends of mint green in the warp. The first square is woven by alternating one pick each of purple and green. The second square is woven by alternating two picks each of purple and green. The third square is woven with all purple weft. The fourth is woven with all green weft. Use your imagination to come up with other combinations in both the warp and weft!

pleasing proportions **bag**

modern art and Scandinavian design offer endless inspiration for weaving. In both disciplines, proportional blocks are utilized beautifully. Tapestry, a weft-faced plain-weave technique, is a great way to place pure color blocks next to one another. Only the weft yarn shows in tapestry (there are no visible interactions between the warp and weft), which makes it easier to choose harmonizing colors. The only trick is to be consistent in how the two colors are handled at the color changes. In this project, the green always lays on top of the brown at the join.

Finished Dimensions
About 7" (18 cm) wide by 8½" (21.5 cm) long, with 42" (106.5 cm) strap.

Weave Structure
Weft-faced tapestry.

Equipment
12-dent rigid heddle with a 7" (18 cm) weaving width; two 8" (20.5 cm) stick shuttles; two 6" (15 cm) stick shuttles; tapestry beater or fork (optional).

Warp and Weft Specifications

Sett (epi)
4 (using a 12-dent rigid heddle).

Weaving Width
7" (18 cm).

Picks per Inch (ppi)
34.

Warp Length
60" (152 cm; includes 30" [76 cm] for loom waste and take-up, and 10" [25.5 cm] for sampling).

Number of Warp Ends
28.

Yarns

Warp
2-ply worsted-weight wool (900 yd [823 m]/lb): 47 yd (43 m) olive green.
Shown here: Harrisville Design Highland (100% wool; 450 yd [411.5 m]/8 oz): Cypress (olive green).

Weft
2-ply worsted-weight wool (900 yd [823 m]/lb): 60 yd (55 m) olive green, 15 yd (13.5 m) forest green, 9 yd (8 m) brown, and 39 yd (35.5 m) brick red. Additional yarn will be needed for sampling.
Shown here: Harrisville Design Highland (100% wool; 450 yd [411.5 m]/8 oz): Cypress (olive green), Evergreen (forest green), Teak (brown), and Russet (brick red).

Strap
60" (152.5 cm) of ⅛" (3 mm) tan leather cord.
2-ply worsted-weight wool (900 yd [823 m]/lb): 8 yd (7.5 m) each forest green, brown, and brick red.
Shown here: Harrisville Design Highland (100% wool; 450 yd [411.5 m]/8 oz): Evergreen (forest green), Teak (brown), and Russet (brick red).

PROJECT NOTES

To pack the weft in tightly, you'll need to use a heavy beat. You may find it helpful to hold the beater firmly against the fell of the cloth as you change the shed. You may also want to use a tapestry beater (a heavy-handled short comb) or fork to pack the weft in tightly.

WARPING

Warp the loom (see page 24), following the specifications on page 89. To space the warp in the reed, *thread a slot, skip the next hole and slot, then thread a hole, skip the next slot and hole, and repeat from * across the width. Every threaded slot must be followed by a threaded hole in order to form plain-weave sheds.

Wind one 8" (20.5 cm) shuttle with olive green and the other with brick red. Wind one 6" (15 cm) shuttle with forest green and the other one with brown (it's easier to weave smaller blocks with shorter shuttles).

WEAVING

Weave 2" (5 cm) of header with a firm beat to spread the warp ends and to provide a ground to beat against (see page 40).

Using the 8" (20.5 cm) shuttle, weave 8½" (21.5 cm) with olive green, using a heavy beat to maintain 34 picks per inch. Change to brick red and weave 5¼" (13.5 cm).

faced fabrics

By making the warp denser than the weft, or vice versa, you can create a bevy of interesting fabrics from sturdy rugs to tapestry bags. The secret is all in the beat.

Weave the Green and Brown Blocks

Step 1: Open the next shed and place the forest green shuttle in the shed from left to right, exiting to the right of the 18th warp thread. Rest this shuttle on the woven cloth. Starting at the right side of the shed, pass the brown shuttle through the same shed to the left of the 10th warp thread from the right and exit to the left of the warp thread. Both wefts will be exiting up through the same space. Rest the shuttle on the woven cloth so that the brown yarn is on top of the forest green weft that has exited the warp. Change the shed and beat.

Step 2: Pick up the forest green shuttle so that it catches the brown yarn and pass it back through the shed from right to left. Pass the brown shuttle through the same shed from left to right. The two wefts will be wound around the same warp end to form a tidy join where the colors meet (see illustration below). Rest the two shuttles on the cloth again, change the shed, and beat.

Repeat Steps 1 and 2 until the blocks measure 3¼" (8.5 cm) tall. As you work, be sure to keep the line between the two colored blocks straight. You can fine-tune the join by gently pulling on the weft threads after the first beat. To readjust, simply open the shed, make the adjustment, then beat. Weave a few picks with scrap yarn to keep the last weft picks in place.

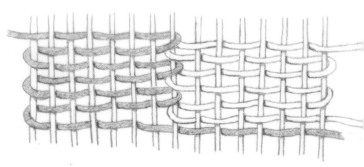

Wrap the two colors of weft around the same warp end to prevent holes at color changes.

FINISHING

Remove the fabric from the loom (see page 46) by untying the warp ends off the back and front apron rods to leave enough length to needle weave the warp ends back into the fabric later. Remove the scrap yarn in the header.

Using a tapestry needle, push each warp end through the space to its left (between it and the adjacent warp end, following the path of the adjacent warp) and exit it through the warp about an inch from the top. Trim the tails close to the cloth.

Fold the cloth in half at the transition between olive green and brick red so that the brown block is on the left side. Using olive green and the baseball stitch (see page 120), sew the sides together, needle weaving the beginning and ending tails back into the fabric. Remove the scrap yarn from the weft.

Washing

If you plan to launder the bag later, gently handwash the fabric in warm water with mild soap. Rinse. Press the fabric between a folded towel to remove excess water. Lay flat to dry.

Strap

Cut two 90" (229 cm) lengths each of forest green, brown, and brick red. Tie these lengths together with one end of the leather cord to the leg of a sturdy table. Be sure you have plenty of room to move back as the braid grows. Using two groups each of one forest green, one brown, and one brick red held together with the leather cord, make a three-strand braid (see page 120) about 45" (114.5 cm) long. Tie an overhand knot to secure the end. Remove the strands from the leg of the table and tie this end into another overhand knot.

Turn the bag inside out and use a whipstitch (see page 121) to sew the strap to one side of the bag above and below the knot on the strap. Repeat on the other side. Trim the ends about 1/4" (6 mm) below the knots.

bamboo obi

the obi is the outermost sash worn with a Japanese kimono. Typically it is quite long and wraps around the body several times. This modernized version uses a color reversal so that you see two different patterns as it wraps around the body. The warp-faced fabric is stiff enough to hold its shape, while the bamboo provides drape and sheen. The patterning is a result of alternating dark and light threads in the warp and weft. Long twisted fringe provides an elegant finished look that enables a knot to be tied without wrinkling the cloth.

Finished Dimensions
About 3¾" (9.5 cm) wide by 62" (157.5 cm) long, with 10½" (26.5 cm) fringe at each end.

Weave Structure
Warp-faced plain weave.

Equipment
12-dent rigid heddle with 4" (10 cm) weaving width; one 4" (10 cm) belt or inkle (beveled-edge) shuttle.

Warp and Weft Specifications

Sett (epi)
12.

Weaving Width
4" (10 cm).

Picks per Inch (ppi)
10.

Warp Length
124" (315 cm; includes 30" [76 cm] for loom waste and take-up, and 10" [25.5 cm] for sampling).

Number of Warp Ends
48.

Warp Color Order
[1 light, 2 dark, 3 light, 5 dark, 3 light, 2 dark] 5 times, end 1 light.

Yarns

Warp
4-ply light worsted-weight (DK) bamboo (1,050 yd [960 m]/lb): 124 yd light green, 155 yd (142 m) dark green.
Shown here: Halcyon Yarn Satin Bamboo (100% bamboo; 200 yd [183 m]/3 oz): #23 (light green) and #24 (dark green).

Weft
4-ply light worsted-weight (DK) bamboo (1,050 yd [960 m]/lb): 42 yd (38.5 m) light green and 42 yd (38.5 m) dark green. Additional yarn will be needed for sampling.
Shown here: Halcyon Yarn Satin Bamboo (100% bamboo; 200 yd [183 m]/3 oz): #23 (light green) and #24 (dark green).
Note: This yarn has been discontinued. Substitute Be Sweet Bamboo (100% bamboo; 110 yd [101 m]/50 g).

PROJECT NOTES

The trick to weaving warp-faced fabric is to use a firm consistent beat that will maintain the cloth's width evenly throughout the weaving process. Use a belt or inkle shuttle that has a beveled edge and that is about the width of your fabric. Instead of beating with the rigid heddle, use the shuttle to press the weft into place. Use the 10" (25.5 cm) of sampling warp to practice your beat.

Pack as much yarn on the shuttle as you can (ideally the entire length of this weft) without interfering with the warp as you weave—joins in warp-faced fabrics are more likely to show. If you can't get all of the yarn on the smaller shuttle, consider using a larger shuttle.

WARPING

Warp the loom (see page 24) following the specifications on page 93.

Wind the dark green on the shuttle, leaving the beveled edge free of yarn (see page 106).

WEAVING

Sampling

Because this is a warp-faced fabric, there's no need to use scrap yarn to spread the warp. Instead, you want the warp to spread as little as possible. In the first shed, bring the yarn to just the point where the warp begins to show gaps from being tied onto the apron rod. Change sheds without bringing the rigid heddle forward, use the sharp edge of the shuttle to press the weft yarn into place. Continue by throwing a pick, changing sheds without bringing the rigid heddle to the fell of the cloth, then pressing the yarn into place. Place the weft at an angle of about 20 degrees (the warp will do most of the bending in the under-over sequence, not the weft). Change sheds, again without bringing the reed to the fell. Then use the sharp edge of the shuttle to press the weft firmly into place. Practice for the length of your sample warp to achieve even tension and straight selvedges.

Advance the warp, leaving a 12" (30.5 cm) gap between the sample and the beginning of the belt fabric (this will be used for fringe). Insert two shots of fine scrap yarn to hold the bamboo picks in place when you cut the cloth from the loom.

Begin weaving with dark green for 31" (78.5 cm) maintaining a firm and even beat. Check the width often and un-weave picks as necessary if the width changes.
Change to light green and weave for 31" (78.5 cm) more. Finish by weaving another two picks with fine scrap yarn.

FINISHING

Remove the fabric from the loom (see page 46), leaving 12" (30.5 cm) of loom waste at each end for fringe. Remove the two picks of scrap yarn.

Fringe

Using two groups of two warp ends at a time, make twisted fringe (see page 121) along each short end of the obi. Tie an overhand knot about 2" (5 cm) from the end of each twisted fringe, taking care to make the knots all the same distance from the cloth. Trim the ends evenly.

It isn't necessary to wash the belt before wearing. When it is time to launder, handwash the belt in lukewarm water with gentle soap. Rinse, then roll in a towel to remove excess moisture. Lay flat to dry.

no two alike **napkins**

one of the joys of being a weaver is putting on a long warp and weaving off a bunch of projects of which no two are the same. For these napkins, you'll weave two sets that mirror each other. The thirsty unmercerized cotton is doubled in the warp and sett closely to give you a sturdy, absorbent cloth with a lot of drape. The twill effect is a phenomenon called tracking that occurs in plain weave. During wet finishing, the raised bumps caused by the warp and weft interactions can be accentuated (depending on the twist and structure of your yarn) to form visual diagonal lines. Tracking isn't something that you can easily control, but it is an added bonus when it appears!

Finished Dimensions
Four napkins, each about 13¼" (33.5 cm) wide by 12½" (31.5 cm) long, with ¼" (6 mm) fringe at each end.

Weave Structure
Warp-dominant plain weave.

Equipment
12-dent rigid heddle with a 15" (38 cm) weaving width; three stick shuttles.

Warp and Weft Specifications
Sett (epi)
12.

Weaving Width
15" (38 cm).

Picks per Inch (ppi)
11.

Warp Length
90" (228.5 cm; includes 18" [45.5 cm] for loom waste and take-up).

Number of Warp Ends
358 (2 ends in every slot and hole).

Warp Color Order
72 natural, 214 teal, 72 natural.

Yarns
Warp
2-ply unmercerized cotton (3,369 yd [3,081 m]/lb): 396 yd (362 m) natural and 590 yd (539 m) teal.

Shown here: Cotton Clouds Aurora Earth (100% cotton; 3,369 yd [3,081 m]/lb): #79 Natural and #68 Duck (teal).

Weft
8/2 unmercerized cotton (3,369 yd [3,081 m]/lb): 124 yd (113 m) natural and 124 yd (113 m) teal.
Shown here: Cotton Clouds Aurora Earth (100% cotton; 3,369 yd [3,081 m]/lb): #79 Natural and #68 Duck (teal).

WARPING

Warp the loom (see page 24), following the specifications on page 97.

WEAVING

Wind natural on one stick shuttle and teal on a second stick shuttle. Wind a generous amount of scrap yarn onto a third stick shuttle.

Weave a few inches of header to spread the warp ends (see page 40).

Weave 15" (38 cm) of teal for the first napkin, then 2" (5 cm) of scrap yarn to allow for fringe, to keep the weft in place when the napkins are cut apart, and to provide a firm foundation for the next napkin.

Weave 15" (38 cm) of natural for the second napkin, then 2" (5 cm) of scrap yarn.

Weave 3" (7.5 cm) of natural, 9" (23 cm) of teal, and 3" (7.5 cm) of natural for the third napkin, then 2" (5 cm) of scrap yarn.

Weave 3" (7.5 cm) of teal, 9" (23 cm) of natural, and 3" (7.5 cm) of teal for the fourth napkin, then 2" (5 cm) of scrap yarn.

FINISHING

Remove the fabric from the loom (see page 46). Cut the napkins apart in the centers of the scrap-yarn bands, leaving the scrap yarn in place. Using a straight stitch, machine stitch each end of each napkin. Remove the scrap yarn. Machine wash the napkins on the gentle cycle with mild soap and tumble dry on the low setting. Remove the napkins from the dryer while still damp, then press until fully dry. Trim the fringe to ¼" (6 mm) using a rotary cutter on a self-healing mat.

simply striped **rug**

simple stripes in rich colors create a floor covering that's perfect for any room. With colored pencils, sketch your stripe sizes and colors on paper until you find an arrangement that works for you. A tapestry beater—a large handheld "fork"—will come in handy when weaving this cloth. You can press the weft into place with the rigid heddle, but the tapestry beater will help pack the weft further to create a dense, sturdy fabric. Lattice knotting finishes the warp ends and adds a decorative touch.

Finished Dimensions
About 19½" (49.5 cm) wide by 34" (86.5 cm) long, with 1" (2.5 cm) fringe at each end.

Weave Structure
Weft-faced plain weave.

Equipment
12-dent rigid heddle with 21" (53.5 cm) weaving width; three stick shuttles; tapestry beater (optional).

Warp and Weft Specifications

Sett (epi)
4 (using a 12-dent rigid heddle).

Weaving Width
21" (53.5 cm).

Picks per Inch (ppi)
21.

Warp Length
68" (173 cm; includes 30" [76 cm] for loom waste and take-up).

Number of Warp Ends
84.

Yarns

Warp
4-ply 8/4 fingering-weight unmercerized cotton (1,600 yd [1,463 m]/lb): 160 yd (181 m) pink.
Shown here: Mayville Carpet Warp (100% cotton; 800 yd [731.5 m]/8 oz): dusty rose.

Weft
2-ply very bulky wool (260 yd [237.5 m]/lb): 57 yd (52 m) maroon, 226 yd (206.5 m) pink, and 212 yd (194 m) rust.
Shown here: Halcyon Yarn Rug Wool (100% wool; 260 yd [237.5 m]/lb): #109 (maroon), #135 (dusty pink), and #106 (rust).

WARPING

Warp the loom (see page 24) following the specifications on page 101. To space the warp in the reed, *thread a slot, skip the next hole and slot, then thread a hole, skip the next slot and hole, and repeat from * across the width. Every threaded slot must be followed by a threaded hole in order to form plain-weave sheds.

Wind one shuttle each with rust, dusty pink, and maroon.

WEAVING

Weave about 3" (7.5 cm) of firmly packed header to spread the warp ends (see page 40) and provide a solid ground for beating the weft.

Using a firm beat to ensure that the warp ends are completely covered with the weft, weave 3" (7.5 cm) with rust, 2" (5 cm) with dusty pink, 1" (2.5 cm) with maroon, then 2" (5 cm) of pink. Repeat this sequence three more times, then weave 3" (7.5 cm) with rust.

Weave 2" (5 cm) of firmly packed header to keep the last weft pick in place.

ply-splitting for seamless joins

Leaving a 5" (12.5 cm) tail, cut the old weft. Ravel the plies of the tail and place them into the next shed. Pull one of the plies to the top of the shed 1" (2.5 cm) from the selvedge. Place the new weft in the shed on the opposite side of the join, also leaving a 5" (12.5 cm) tail. Beat the weft in place, then change sheds. Ravel the plies of the new tail and tuck them into this shed, then pull one of the plies to the top of shed 1" (2.5 cm) from the selvedge. Beat the weft in place. Continue to weave as usual for a few inches, then trim the loose plies close to the fabric.

FINISHING

Remove the fabric from the loom (see page 46), leaving several inches of warp at each end for fringe. Place the rug on a table so that about 1" (2.5 cm) of woven rug hangs over the edge. Carefully remove the header, disturbing the weft as little as possible.

Fringe

Starting at one edge, tie the first and second warp ends together in an overhand knot as close to the edge of the cloth as possible. Continue across the width, tying together every two warp ends. You may have to push the warp up at times to keep the edge of the cloth even.

Starting with the second and third warp ends, tie a second row of overhand knots ½" (1.3 cm) below the first knot so that the second row of knots is offset from the first by one warp end. Using a rotary cutter against a self-healing mat, trim the warp ½" (1.3 cm) from the second set of knots.

The rug does not have to be washed before use. If it becomes dirty, soak it in a bathtub in lukewarm water with mild soap. Use a soft scrub brush to loosen any dirt. Rinse, then roll in a towel to remove excess water. Lay flat to dry.

pick-up **belt**

using a pick-up stick, you can create a whole new array of patterns in your cloth. The stick holds warp threads above or below the shed to form warp or weft "floats" across the other threads to create a third shed. Pick-up techniques have been used by every culture that has a weaving tradition, as it is an intuitive step in creating pattern with a simple loom. In this cloth, the warp is raised in a simple pattern that results in a weft-faced fabric that's perfect for a belt.

Finished Dimensions
About 1½" (3.8 cm) wide by 41" (104 cm) long.

Weave Structure
Plain weave with pick-up.

Equipment
10-dent rigid heddle with 2" (5 cm) weaving width; pick-up stick; beveled belt or inkle shuttle.

Notions
Two 1¼" (3.2 cm) wide by 1½" (3.8 cm) tall rectangular metal buckles; Fray Check.

Warp and Weft Specifications

Sett (epi)
10.

Weaving Width
2" (5 cm).

Picks per Inch (ppi)
32.

Warp Length
82" (208 cm; includes 30" [76 cm] for loom waste and take-up; 10" [25.5 cm] for sampling).

Number of Warp Ends
19.

Yarns

Warp
Worsted-weight wool (988 yd [903.5 m]/lb): 44 yd (40 m) teal.
Shown here: Brown Sheep Cotton Fleece (80% cotton, 20% merino wool; 215 yd [196 m]/3½ oz): CW-450 Oriental Jade.

Weft
Worsted-weight wool (988 yd [903.5 m]/lb): 83 yd (76 m) purple. Additional yarn will be needed for sampling.
Shown here: Brown Sheep Cotton Fleece (80% cotton, 20% merino wool; 215 yd [196 m]/3½ oz): #CW-730 Raging Purple.

Buckle
Worsted-weight wool (988 yd [903.5 m]/lb): 3 yd teal.
Shown here: Brown Sheep Cotton Fleece (80% cotton, 20% merino wool; 215 yd [196 m]/3½ oz): #CW-450 Oriental Jade.

WARPING

Warp the loom (see page 24) following the specifications on page 105, placing the first and last warp end in a slot on the rigid heddle.

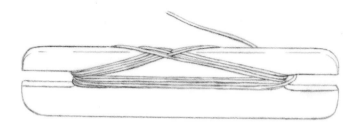

Wind the beveled shuttle with purple, being careful not to wind yarn on the beveled edge.

WEAVING

Weave an inch or two of header to spread the warp ends (see page 40).

Leaving an 8" (20.5 cm) tail for hemstitching later, weave 2" (5 cm) with purple. Thread the tail on a tapestry needle and use it to hemstitch (see page 120) over two warps and two wefts. Work the pick-up pattern as shown at right.

FINISHING

Remove the fabric from the loom (see page 46). Remove the waste yarn from the header. Apply Fray Check to the hemstitching.

Thread teal on a tapestry needle. Starting at the center of one long side, work buttonhole stitches (see page 120) around each metal rectangle, leaving a 2" (5 cm) tail of yarn at each end. Tie the two tails together in an overhand knot. Apply Fray Check to the knot and snip the ends when dry.

With the float side up, place the plain-weave section through both rectangles so that the knots are encased in the fabric. Sew the tab of plain weave to the back of the belt so that it holds both loops.

Work pick-up pattern as follows:

Step 1: Place the rigid heddle in the down position so that only the slot threads are up.

Step 2: Using a pick-up stick and working behind the rigid heddle, pick up every other warp thread. These will be the ends threaded through the slots.

Step 3: Put the rigid heddle in the neutral position.

Step 4: Turn the pick-up stick toward the back of the loom on its side, thereby creating a new shed.

Step 5: Weave three picks in the same shed, taking care to catch the selvedge threads with each pass and using the shuttle to press each pick in place.

Step 6: Slide the pick-up stick toward the back of the loom to rest on the back beam so that it doesn't interfere with the normal sheds.

Step 7: Place the rigid heddle in the up position and weave three picks of plain weave, changing sheds with each pick (up, down, up) and using the rigid heddle to beat the picks firmly to achieve 32 ppi.

Repeat Steps 3–7 until 42" (106.5 cm) has been woven, ending in 3 picks of plain weave. Cut the weft, leaving an 8" (20.5 cm) tail. Thread the tail on a tapestry needle and hemstitch as before.

weaving pick-up

1. Place the rigid heddle in the down position.

2. Use a pick-up stick to lift every other raised warp end.

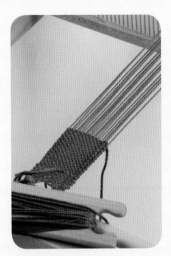

3. Bring the rigid heddle to the neutral position.

4. Turn the pick-up stick on its side to create a new shed.

5. Weave one pick.

6. Wrap the selvedge and weave another pick.

7. Beat each pick with the beveled edge of the shuttle.

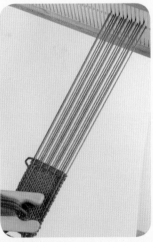

8. Rest the pick-up stick on the back beam and weave three picks of plain weave.

space-saving **mats**

at times, being spacey can be a good thing. The spaces in these mats are formed by skipping holes and slots while the warp is threaded through the rigid heddle to create a lacy look while economizing on warp yarn. All four of these mats are woven on the same warp, but a different hue is used for the weft of each for visual variety. To keep the yarns from slipping, the first and last weft picks held in place with a fray blocker such as Fray Check, requiring no further finishing than trimming the fringe.

Finished Dimensions
Four mats, each about 14" (35.5 cm) wide by 19" (48.5 cm) long, with 2" (5 cm) fringe at each end.

Weave Structure
Plain weave with spaced warp.

Equipment
10-dent rigid heddle with 15" (38 cm) weaving width; one stick shuttle; three 4" (10 cm) cardboard spacers a little longer than the weaving width.

Warp and Weft Specifications
Sett (epi)
10.

Weaving Width
15" (38 cm).

Picks per Inch (ppi)
10.

Warp Length
122" (310 cm; includes 30" [76 cm] for loom waste and take-up, and 4" [10 cm] between mats for fringe).

Number of Warp Ends
84.

Warp Spacing Order
[Thread 6, skip 12, thread 6, skip 3, thread 12, skip 3] 3 times, thread 6, skip 12, thread 6.

Yarns
Warp
2-ply 3/2 mercerized cotton (1,260 yd [1,152 m]/lb): 285 yd [260.5 m] yellow gold.

Shown here: UKI 3/2 Mercerized Cotton Yarn (100% cotton; 1,260 yd [1,152 m]/lb): #30 Antique.

Weft
2-ply 3/2 mercerized cotton (1,260 yd [1,152 m]/lb): 92 yd (84 m) each of four shades of gold.

Shown here: UKI 3/2 Mercerized Cotton Yarn (100% cotton; 1,260 yd [1,152 m]/lb): #84 Gold Dust, #9 Ginger, #7 Oak, and #29 Old Gold.

Other Supplies
Fray Check.

WARPING

Warp the loom (see page 24) following the specifications on page 109. Be sure to double-check the spacings in the threading—mistakes will show!

WEAVING

Weave an inch or two header to spread the warp ends (see page 40).

With your first weft color, weave a pick, change sheds, tuck the tail from the first pick into the new shed and throw the second pick, beating the tail between the two weft picks. Weave a few more inches, then apply Fray Check to the end of the cloth to prevent the warp and weft threads from drifting. Allow the Fray Check to thoroughly dry before advancing the warp. Continue to weave for a total of 20" (51 cm). Cut the weft, leaving an 8" (21.5 cm) tail. Thread the tail on a tapestry needle and needle weave (see page 120) it into the cloth between the second-to-last and the last pick and exit in front of the last warp end before the first gap. Apply Fray Check to the exit point of the weft tail and allow it to dry thoroughly, then trim the tails.

Insert a 4" (10 cm) cardboard spacer between the end of the first mat and the beginning of the second. With a different weft color, weave another mat in the same way, being careful that the first few picks form a straight edge. Weave two more mats with the remaining two weft colors.

FINISHING

Remove the fabric from the loom (see page 46), leaving several inches of warp at each end for fringe. Remove the header and spacers.

Carefully cut apart the mats in the center of the 4" (10 cm) unwoven spacings with a rotary cutter against a self-healing mat, leaving 2" (5 cm) of fringe at each side of each mat.

To launder the mats, handwash them in warm water with dish soap and lay flat to dry. Fray Check is water resistant under mild temperatures.

lovely lace

Any structure that creates open spaces in weaving can be considered lace. Lace can be as simple as using a loose sett with fine thread, as in the Layered Cravat on page 77, or skipping spaces in the warp or weft , as in these mats. There are also lovely hand-manipulated weaves that twist the warp or weft in decorative ways to make unique gauzy fabrics, as in the Leno Runner on page 113 or the Bouquet Shawl on page 117.

leno **runner**

linen and leno are a natural combination. Linen, which comes from stiff plant fibers derived from the flax plant, provides a crisp finished look and high sheen. Fabrics woven from this fiber are called "linens." Leno is a form of lace where crossed warp threads are held in place by the weft. Use your fingers to cross the threads, then hold them in place with a pick-up stick while the weft is thrown to secure them in position. Simple to do, leno adds a decorative look to simple fabrics. The more rows of leno you work, the lacier the look.

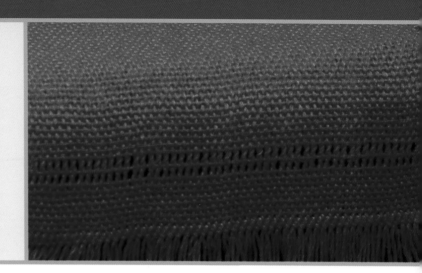

Finished Dimensions
About 10¼" (26 cm) wide by 35" (89 cm) long, with 2" (5 cm) fringe at each end.

Weave Structure
Plain weave with leno.

Equipment
10-dent rigid heddle with 11" (28 cm) weaving width; one stick shuttle; one pick-up stick.

Warp and Weft Specifications

Sett (epi)
10.

Weaving Width
10¾" (27.5 cm).

Picks per Inch (ppi)
6.

Warp Length
63" (160 cm; includes 24" [61 cm] for loom waste and take-up). *Note: The loom waste is calculated as fringe to allow just one skein for the warp.*

Number of Warp Ends
108.

Yarns

Warp
Worsted-weight wet-spun linen (870 yd [795.5 m]/lb): 190 yd (173.5 m) red. *Shown here:* Louet North America Euroflax Wet-Spun Linen (100% linen; 190 yd [173.5 m]/100 g): #11 Red.

Weft
Worsted-weight wet-spun linen (870 yd [795.5 m]/lb): 80 yd (73 m) berry red. *Shown here:* Louet North America Euroflax Wet-Spun Linen (100% linen; 70 yd [64 m]/100 g): #23 Berry Red.

WARPING

Warp the loom (see page 24) following the specifications on page 113.

Wind a shuttle with the entire length of weft.

WEAVING

Weave an inch or two header to spread the warp ends (see page 40).

Leaving a 40" (101.5 cm) tail for hemstitching later, work plain weave for 1½" (3.8 cm). Thread the tail on a tapestry needle and hemstitch (see page 120) over two warps and two wefts.

Work one row of leno following the instructions at right.

Weave 35" (89 cm), then work another row of leno, then work plain weave for 1½" (3.8 cm). Cut the weft, leaving a 40" (101.5 cm) tail and hemstitch as before.

FINISHING

Remove the fabric from the loom (see page 46), leaving several inches of warp at each end for fringe. Remove the header.

Handwash the fabric in lukewarm water with delicate soap. Rinse. Roll in a towel to squeeze out excess moisture and lay flat to dry.

Using a rotary cutter against a self-healing mat, trim the fringe to 2" (5 cm).

leno

Leno is worked by crossing the warp threads over one another in groups of two. It can be worked on an open or closed (shown here) shed. For beginners, I find that it's easier to work on a closed shed. The instructions here are for working 1:1 leno in a single row.

Step 1: Working from the right, pull the edge warp end up and over the warp end to the left.

Step 2: Slip a pick-up stick between the crossed warp threads to hold them in place.

Step 3: Cross the next warp end over its neighbor and slip the pick-up stitch between them. Continue in this manner across the entire width of the warp.

Step 4: Rotate the pick-up stick on its side to create a new shed and pass the shuttle in front of the pick-up stick.

Step 5: Push the pick-up stick to the fell of the cloth to straighten the twists, then remove the pick-up stick.

Step 6: Look to see how the last plain-weave pick was woven—up or down—and weave the next pick in the same shed. If the last pick was up, weave an up shed. If the last pick was down, weave a down shed.

working leno lace

1. Lift and cross the edge warp end over adjacent warp end.

2. Insert the pick-up stick between the crossed warp ends.

3. Cross the next two warp ends and insert the stick between them.

4. Cross adjacent warp ends across the entire warp width.

5. Turn the pick-up stick on its side to create a new shed, then pass the shuttle through this shed.

6. Push the pick-up stick to the fell to beat the weft and to straighten the twists.

7. Change the shed and weave another pick as usual.

8. Pack the weft with the rigid heddle.

brooks bouquet **shawl**

wrapping weft around groups of warp threads creates a lovely lace pattern on plain-weave fabric. In this shawl, a small shuttle is used to wrap the weft around groups of eight warp ends after every five picks of plain weave are woven. The result is a honeycomb-type texture that looks much more complicated than it really is. The key to making beautiful fabric is to maintain constant tension in the weft. Combine this technique with soft luxury yarns to create a stunning wrap for chilly evenings.

Finished Dimensions
About 15" (38 cm) wide by 68" (173 cm) long, with 6½" (16.5 cm) fringe at each end.

Weave Structure
Plain weave with Brooks bouquet variation.

Equipment
10-dent rigid heddle with 20" (51 cm) weaving width; one 18" (45.5 cm) stick shuttle; one 4" (10 cm) stick shuttle.

Warp and Weft Specifications

Sett (epi)
10.

Weaving Width
20" (51 cm).

Picks per Inch (ppi)
6.

Warp Length
114" (290 cm; includes 30" [76 cm] for loom waste and take-up).

Number of Warp Threads
200.

Yarns

Warp
4-ply worsted-weight wool/microfiber acrylic/cashmere blend (896 yd [819 m]/lb): 634 yd (580 m) olive green.
Shown here: Cascade Yarns Cash Vero (55% merino, 33% microfiber acrylic, 12% cashmere; 98 yd [89.5 m]/50 g): #031 olive green.

Weft
4-ply worsted-weight wool/microfiber acrylic/cashmere blend (896 yd [819 m]/lb): 318 yd (291 m) olive green.
Shown here: Cascade Yarns Cash Vero (55% merino, 33% microfiber acrylic, 12% cashmere; 98 yd [89.5 m]/50 g): #031 olive green.
Note: This yarn has been discontinued. Substitute Debbie Bliss Cashmerino Aran (55% merino, 33% microfiber acrylic, 12% cashmere; 99 yd [91 m]/50 g).

PROJECT NOTES

This warp yarn has a lot of give, so be sure to wind it loosely when measuring the warp on the warping board; otherwise you might end up with a shorter warp than you planned.

WARPING

Wind the warp in two groups of 100 threads each.

Warp the loom (see page 24) following the specifications on page 117 and threading the first warp end in a slot.

WEAVING

Weave an inch or two header to spread the warp ends (see page 40).

Leaving a 100" (254 cm) tail, weave five picks. Wind the tail on a short shuttle and work a row of Brooks bouquet (at right). Work another row of Brooks bouquet at the end of the five picks already woven. Continue to alternate five picks of plain weave with a row of Brooks bouquet until the piece measures 84" (213 cm), ending with a row of Brooks bouquet.

FINISHING

Remove the fabric from the loom (see page 46), allowing 6½" (16.5 cm) of loom waste to be used as fringe at each end.

Gently handwash the shawl in lukewarm water and delicate soap. Roll it in a towel to remove excess water and lay it flat to dry.

Using a rotary cutting against a self-healing mat, trim the fringe to 6½" (16.5 cm) at each end.

This is a variation of the traditional Brooks bouquet pattern.

Step 1: With the shed in the up position and starting at the right selvedge, pass the shuttle under the first four lifted warp ends.

Step 2: Bring the shuttle through the top of the shed.

Step 3: Pass the shuttle back to the right, bring it under the warp, and exit it in the same place as before. eight threads are encased. (In traditional Brooks bouquet, the yarn is only wrapped around the four up ends. Try both and see which one you like.)

Repeat Steps 1–3 across the entire width of the warp, maintaining even tension on the weft yarn and allowing the weft to travel at a 20-degree angle.

Bring the rigid heddle to the fell of the cloth to even up the wraps, then weave the desired number of picks of plain weave. Alternate rows of Brooks bouquet with plain weave as desired.

weaving bouquets

1. Pass the shuttle under first 4 warp ends.

2. Bring the shuttle through to the top of the shed.

3. Pass the shuttle to right, bring it under the shed, then back up where it exited before.

4. Pass the shuttle under the next 4 warp threads.

5. Wrap the warp in bundles of eight across the entire width.

6. Use the rigid heddle to even up the wrapped bundles.

7. Weave the desired number of picks of plain weave, then work another row of wraps.

illustrated techniques

BASEBALL STITCH

Thread seaming yarn on a tapestry needle. Butt the selvedge edges of two pieces of fabric together or place them back to back. Working from bottom to top, *bring threaded needle from back to front near the edge of one side, then from back to front near the edge of the other side. Repeat from *, inserting the needle a short distance above the previous path.

BUTTONHOLE STITCH

Thread stitching yarn on a tapestry needle. Working from right to left, *bring under the edge of the cloth to be covered, then out again a short distance away, being careful to bring the needle out on top of the stitching yarn. Repeat from * for the desired length.

HEMSTITCHING

Thread weft yarn on a tapestry needle. Working from right to left, *bring the threaded needle under the desired number of warp ends (two shown here) above the fell, then back to the starting point, encircling the group. Pass the needle under the same group of ends, bringing it out through the weaving the desired

number of weft picks below the fell (two shown here). Repeat from * across the fell. To end, needle weave the tail into the cloth and trim the end.

NEEDLE WEAVING

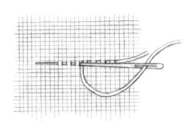

Thread the yarn to be needle-woven on a tapestry needle. Bring the needle in and out of the woven cloth, mimicking the over-under path of one warp end (if working vertically) or one weft pick (if working horizontally) in the woven cloth.

THREE-STRAND BRAID

Cut three strands (or three groups of strands) about two times the desired finished length. Tie the strands together at one end in an overhand knot. *Lay the right strand over the middle strand so that the right strand is now the middle strand. Lay the left strand over the new middle strand. Repeat from * to the desired length.

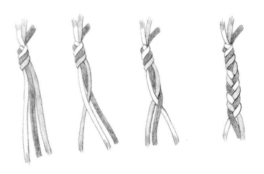

TWISTED FRINGE

Divide the number of strands for each fringe into two groups. Twist each group clockwise until it kinks. Bring both groups together and twist them counterclockwise (allow them to untwist around each other in that direction). Secure the ends with an overhand knot to prevent untwisting.

WHIPSTITCH

Thread seaming yarn on a tapestry needle. Hold the pieces to be seamed together with their wrong sides facing together. *Bring threaded needle through both layers from back to front. Repeat from *, inserting the needle a short distance above the previous path.

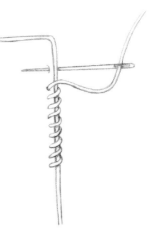

project planning cards

Photocopy this page and keep record of your projects on these handy cards.

PROJECT_____

Warp yarn and length _____

_____

Weft yarn and length _____

_____

Sett _____ Width in the reed _____ PPI _____

Woven dimensions off loom _____
After washing _____

Finishing Techniques _____
_____

PROJECT_____

Warp yarn and length _____

_____

Weft yarn and length _____

_____

Sett _____ Width in the reed _____ PPI _____

Woven dimensions off loom _____
After washing _____

Finishing Techniques _____
_____

terms to know

"Language is the source of misunderstandings."
—*Antoine de Saint Exupery*

One of the biggest challenges to learning anything new is mastering the language. This list will help you understand weaving lingo.

Advance the warp Release tension on the cloth and wind the woven cloth onto the front beam, then re-tension the warp to continue weaving.

Balanced plain weave A fabric in which there is the same number of warp ends and weft picks per inch.

Beat Bring the rigid heddle to the fell of the cloth to align and pack the weft.

Beater Device used to position each weft pick. This is the same as the rigid heddle on a rigid-heddle loom.

Bloom The expansion of yarn once washed and the fibers relax.

Count system Yarn classification system based on the number of yards in a pound of a standard size.

Cross Formed when winding a warp on a warping board. Keeps the warp threads in order and minimizes tangles when threading the loom.

Dressing the loom The process of measuring the warp and winding it on the loom.

End (warp end) One strand of warp.

Ends per inch (epi) The number of warp threads in an inch.

Fell The part of the cloth where the weaving action occurs. The last laid pick.

Felt To agitate scaled fibers so that they fuse together.

Float Where a weft pick or warp end doesn't travel in the normal over-under-over path.

Fringe The unwoven warp that is intentionally left at the ends of woven cloth.

Full Wash and agitate the fabric so that the yarn blooms, and in some cases, shrinks.

Grist The size of a yarn.

Hand The way the cloth feels.

Header The first inch or two of weaving (usually with scrap yarn) to spread out the warp ends to their full weaving width.

Heddles The molded plastic pieces in the rigid heddle through which the warp ends are threaded.

Hemstitching A way to secure the first and last weft picks of cloth (see page 120).

Leader yarn An inelastic yarn that marks the desired path to follow when measuring the warp on the warping board.

Loom waste The amount of extra yarn left over after weaving.

Pick (or shot) One pass of the shuttle through the shed.

Picks per inch (ppi) The number of weft picks in an inch of woven cloth.

Plain weave Cloth woven so that one weft pick travels over/under the warp.

Plied yarn Yarn made up of two or more singles yarn.

Rigid heddle In a shaft loom, the reed is a separate piece of equipment. The rigid-heddle loom incorporates both "rigid" heddles—they are loose on a shaft loom—and reed into one. The reed determines the spacing of the warp.

Selvedges The edge of the cloth where the weft exits one shed and enters the next.

Sett The spacing of the warp ends in the heddle.

Shed The open space that is created when the heddle is lifted up or down.

Shed blocks Used to hold the rigid heddle in the up or down position to produce a shed.

Shot See pick.

Shuttle Used to pass the weft yarn back and forth as you weave.

Singles A single strand of spun fiber.

Stick shuttle A flat shuttle typically used when weaving on rigid-heddle looms.

Take-up The extra amount needed to allow for the weft to bend over and under the warp threads.

Threads Used interchangeably with "yarn" to describe the warp or weft.

Throw To pass the shuttle into the shed.

Warp Threads held taut on a loom and the act of dressing the loom.

Warp dominant Cloth in which the warp ends completely cover the weft picks.

Warp-emphasis weave Cloth in which there are more warp ends per inch than weft picks.

Warp end An individual warp yarn or thread.

Warping board Device used to make it easy to measure the warp ends in preparation for threading the loom when using the indirect warping method.

Warping peg Used to hold the warp during direct warping.

Weave The process of crossing taut warp threads with a weft thread.

Weft The yarn that is passed through the shed of a warped loom and beaten into place.

Weft dominant Cloth in which the weft picks completely cover the warp ends.

Weft-emphasis weave Cloth in which there are more weft picks per inch than warp ends.

Wraps per inch (wpi) The number of times a yarn can be wrapped around a rigid object in an inch.

warping checklist

Photocopy this page for each project and check off your progress.

DIRECT WARPING CHECKLIST

Step One
- ❒ Secure loom and place warping peg at a warp-length distance from the front of the loom.

- ❒ Tie warp yarn onto apron rod, making sure that the apron rod is over the back beam (if your loom has one).

- ❒ Using moderate tension and remembering to center your warp, pull a loop of yarn through the first slot and walk it down to loop over the warping peg.

- ❒ Return to the loom, then repeat this process until the full width of the warp is threaded in the slots.

Step Two
- ❒ Remove the loops from the peg and cut the ends, tie the warp in an overhand knot, then allow it to rest on a table or drop to the floor.

- ❒ Laying smooth paper between the layers of warp, wind the warp onto the back beam, stopping every so often to move to the front of the loom and pull on the warp as a whole to take up any slack.

- ❒ Stop when the warp is positioned to tie onto the front apron rod.

Step Three
- ❒ Check to make sure that you have two warp ends in every desired slot. Make adjustments if necessary.

- ❒ Remove one warp end from each slot and thread it through the adjacent hole.

Step Four
- ❒ Making sure that the apron rod is over the front beam (if your loom has one), tie the warp onto the apron rod.

- ❒ Adjust tension as necessary.

- ❒ Turn the back brake a few times to fully tension the loom.

Your loom is warped! Weave on!

project planning sheet

Photocopy this page and keep record of your warp and weft calculations for every project. *Note:* For take-up and shrinkage, use 10% for cotton-like yarns and 15% for wool-like yarns. Always round up to the nearest whole number.

PROJECT _____

Yarn Selection:

Wraps per inch _____ ÷ 2 = sett _____ (Note: If your heddle has ten dents per inch, you want a yarn that wraps about twenty times per inch for balanced plain weave. *I recommend rounding up as you work.*)

Warp Length:

_____" (woven length of project) + 10–15% (take-up and shrinkage) = _____" + 24" (loom waste) = _____+ 10" (for sampling if desired) = _____" length of each warp thread.

Total Number of Warp Threads Needed:

_____" (woven width of project) + 10–15% (take-up and shrinkage) = _____" (width in the reed) × (number of ends per inch or sett) = _____ number of warp threads.

Amount of Yarn Needed for Warp:

_____ (number of warp threads) × _____" (warp length) = _____" ÷ 36 = _____' (the amount of yarn needed for warp in yards).

Amount of Yarn Needed for Weft:

_____" (width of warp in reed) + 10% (take-up) × _____ (picks per inch)= _____" × _____" (total length of woven warp) = _____ ÷ 36 = _____' (the amount of yarn needed for weft in yards).

Finishing technique _____

Yarn Sample _____ **Source** _____

Yarn Sample _____ **Source** _____

Yarn Sample _____ **Source** _____

Notes _____

sett chart

This list includes scans of each of the yarns used in *Weaving Made Easy*. Underneath each scan you will find the yards per pound (and meters per kilogram) along with a recommended sett for balanced plain weave. Keep in mind that some of the setts may differ from the way they are used in the projects if denser or looser setts were used to weave warp- or weft-emphasis or lacy fabrics. You can use the scans to compare yarns you have on hand and make substitutions. When substituting yarns, it is a good idea to use similar fiber types with the same yarn characteristics. *Handwoven* magazine, published by Interweave, has complied a list of hundreds of yarns and their setts. You'll find their Master Yarn Chart at www.weavingtoday.com/media/p/70.aspx.

COTTON

4-ply bulky-weight unmercerized cotton; 400 yd/lb (810 m/kg); 8

2-ply 3/2 mercerized (pearl) cotton; 1,260 yd/lb (2,444 m/kg); 10

2-ply 8/4 fingering-weight unmercerized cotton; 1,600 yd/lb (3,390 m/kg); 12

2-ply 8/2 unmercerized cotton; 3,369 yd/lb (6,792 m/kg); 6

2-ply 10/2 mercerized (pearl) cotton; 4,000 yd/lb (8,475 m/kg); 24

4-ply worsted-weight unmercerized cotton; 792 yd/lb (1,598 m/kg); 6

WOOL

2-ply very bulky wool; 260 yd/lb (525 m/kg); 4

Heavy worsted-weight singles wool; 630 yd/lb (1,271 m/kg); 8

2-ply worsted-weight wool; 900 yd/lb (1,816 m/kg); 8

3-ply worsted-weight wool; 1,000 yd/lb (2,010 m/kg); 10

2-ply sportweight wool; 1,700 yd/lb (3,431 m/kg); 10

2-ply 28/2 fingering-weight wool; 2,240 yd/lb (4,520 m/kg); 15

BLENDS

2-ply alpaca/wool/metallic blend; 1,250 yd/lb (2,522 m/kg); 10

4-ply wool/silk blend; 1,150 yd/lb (2,230 m/kg);10

Bulky singles wool/mohair/cashmere blend; 1,097 yd/lb (2,213 m/kg); 10

4-ply worsted-weight wool/microfiber acrylic/cashmere blend; 896 yd/lb (1,808 m/kg); 10

2-ply laceweight kid mohair/merino wool/microfiber blend; 5,000 yd/lb (10,100 m/kg); 10

2-ply 18/2 wool/silk blend; 5,040 yd/lb (10,170 m/kg); 24

OTHER FIBERS

4-ply light worsted-weight (DK) bamboo; 1,050 yd/lb (2,113 m/kg); 10

3-ply worsted-weight wet-spun linen; 870 yd/lb; (1,756 m/kg); 10

sources for supplies

SOURCES FOR YARNS

Companies with a * are wholesale only. Contact these companies for a retail source in your area.

*Brown Sheep Company
100662 County Rd. 16
Mitchell, NE 69375
brownsheep.com

*Cascade Yarns
PO Box 58168
1224 Andover Park East
Tukwila, WA 98188
cascadeyarns.com

Crystal Palace
160 23rd St.
Richmond, CA 94804
straw.com/cpy

Cotton Clouds
5176 S. Fourteenth Ave.
Safford, AZ 85546
cottonclouds.com

Diamond Yarn
9697 St. Laurent, Ste. 101
Montreal, QC
Canada H3L 2N1
diamondyarn.com

Halcyon Yarn
12 School St.
Bath, ME 04530
halcyonyarn.com

Harrisville Designs
Center Village
PO Box 806
Harrisville, NH 03450
harrisville.com

*JaggerSpun
PO Box 188
Springvale, ME 04083
jaggerspun.com

Lion Brand Yarn
135 Kero Road
Carlstadt, NJ 07072
lionbrand.com

Louet North America
808 Commerce Park Dr.
Ogdensburg, NY 13669
louet.com
in Canada:
RR #4
Prescott, ON K0E 1T0

Lunatic Fringe
15009 Cromartie Rd.
Tallahassee, FL 32309
lunatic@talstar.com

*Design Source/Manos del Uruguay
PO Box 770
Medford, MA 02155

*Mountain Colors
PO Box 156
Corvallis, MT 59828
mountaincolors.com

*Westminster Fibers/ Nashua/Rowan
165 Ledge St.
Nashua, NH 03060
westminsterfibers.com
in Canada: Diamond Yarn

*Universal Yarns
284 Ann St.
Concord, NC 28025

*UKI
PO Box 848
Hickory, NC 28603

SOURCES FOR LOOMS

*Foxglove Fiberarts Supply/Ashford Looms
8040 NE Day Rd., Bldg. 4, Ste. F
Bainbridge Island, WA 98110
(877) 369-4568
foxglovefiber.com

Glimakra USA
50 Hall Ln.
Clancy, MT 59634
(866) 890-7314
glimakrausa.com

Harrisville Designs
PO Box 806
Harrisville, NH 03450
(603) 827-3333
harrisville.com

*Leclerc Looms
1573 Savoie C.P. 4
Plessisville, QC
Canada G6L 2Y6
(819) 362-2408
leclerclooms.com

*Majacraft Limited
586 Oropi Road, RD3
Tauranga, New Zealand
64 (7) 543-3618
majacraft.com.nz

*New Voyager Trading
212 West Jackson St.
Thomasville, GA 31792
(229) 227-1322
mail@kromskina.com

*Schacht Spindle Co.
6101 Ben Pl.
Boulder, CO 80301
(303) 442-3212
schachtspindle.com

index